THE MEN'S LOCKER ROOM

MILTON BOLZENDAHL

THE MEN'S LOCKER ROOM

© Copyright 2012, R. Milton Bolzendahl

All Rights Reserved.

No part of this book may be reproduced, stored in a
retrieval system, or transmitted by any means,
electronic, mechanical, photocopying, recording,
or otherwise, without written permission
from the author.

ISBN: 978-1-60414-542-7

Published by Fideli Publishing Inc.
www.FideliPublishing.com

THE MEN'S LOCKER ROOM

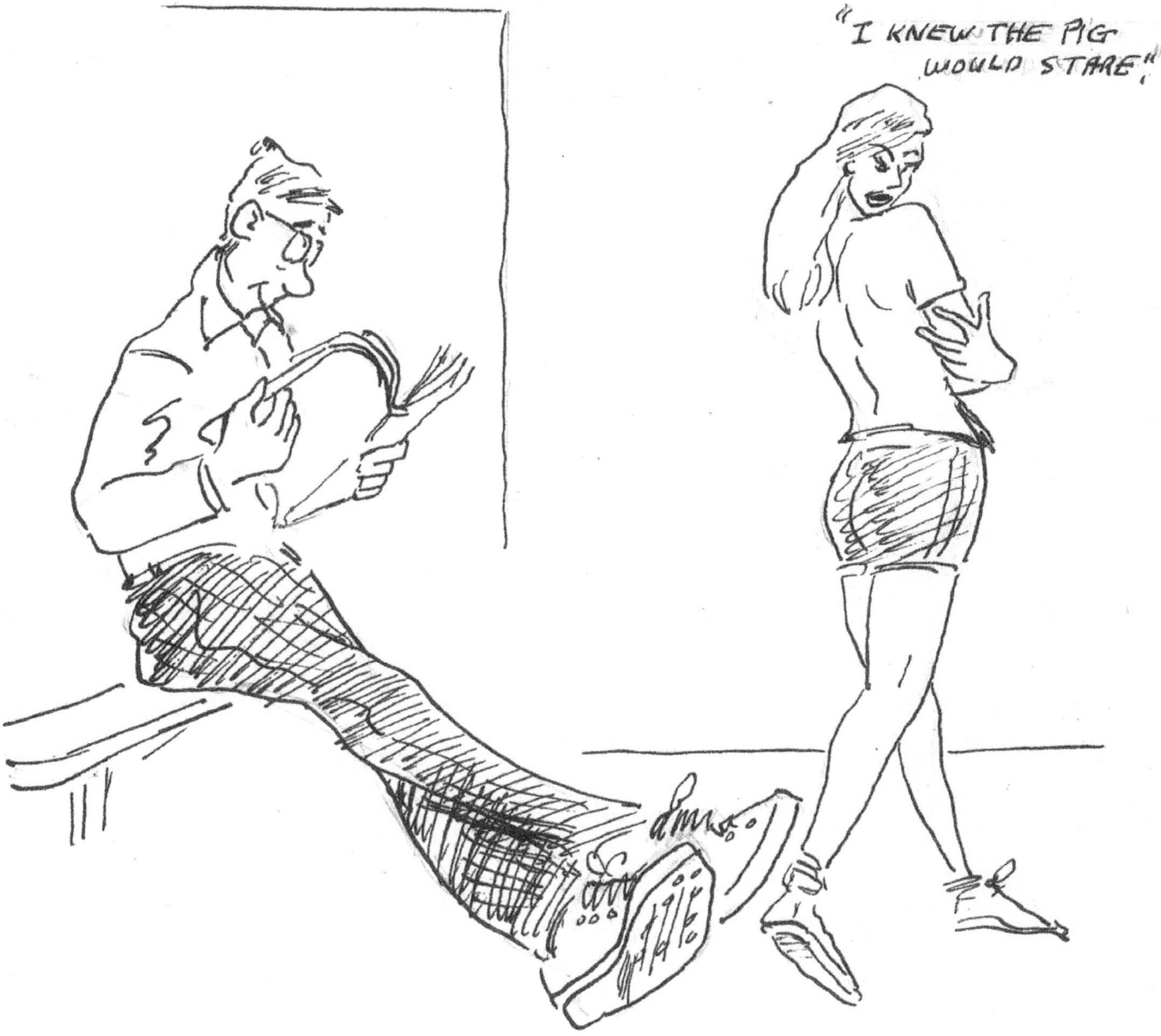
"I KNEW THE PIG WOULD STARE!"

THE MEN'S LOCKER ROOM

DEDICATED

TO MEL BROOKS AND PROFESSOR BARRY HYMAN FOR THEIR UNDYING EFFORT TO SAVE THE ENDANGERED WORD OF LITERARY GREATNESS, "SCHMUCK".

● ● ● ●

IF ANY READER CAN DISCOVER A REASON FOR THIS BOOK, PLEASE LET ME KNOW.

M.B.

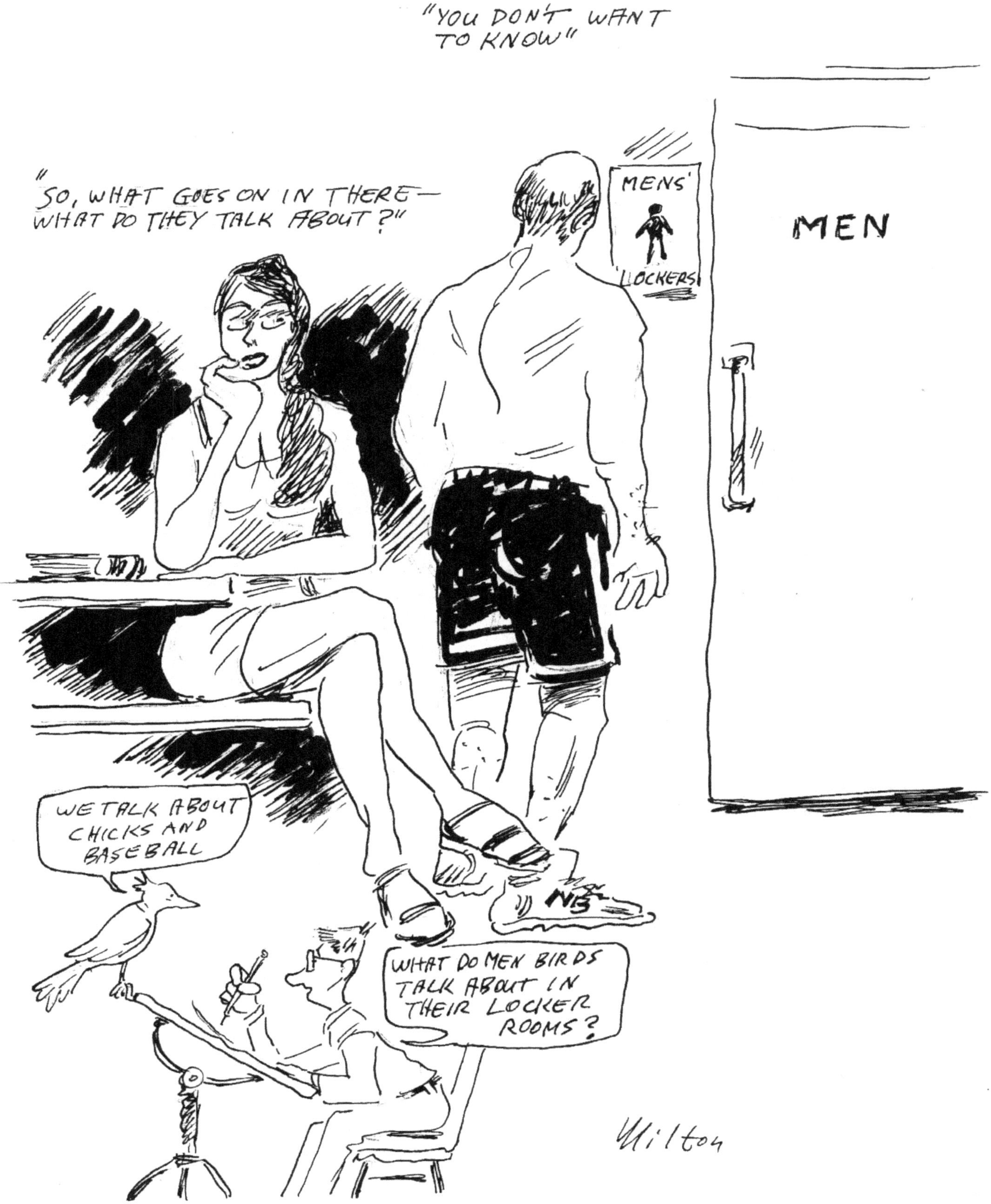
"YOU DON'T WANT TO KNOW"
"SO, WHAT GOES ON IN THERE— WHAT DO THEY TALK ABOUT?"
MENS' LOCKERS
MEN
WE TALK ABOUT CHICKS AND BASEBALL
WHAT DO MEN BIRDS TALK ABOUT IN THEIR LOCKER ROOMS?
NB
Milton

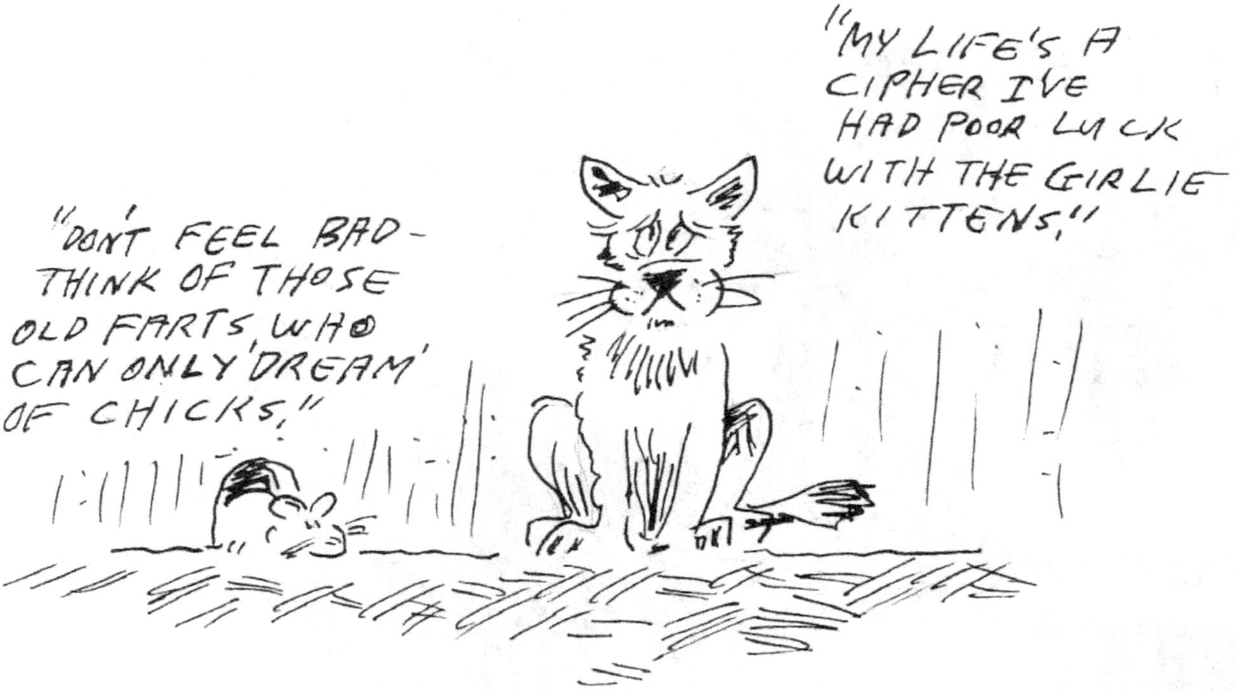
"DON'T FEEL BAD - THINK OF THOSE OLD FARTS, WHO CAN ONLY 'DREAM' OF CHICKS."
"MY LIFE'S A CIPHER I'VE HAD POOR LUCK WITH THE GIRLIE KITTENS."

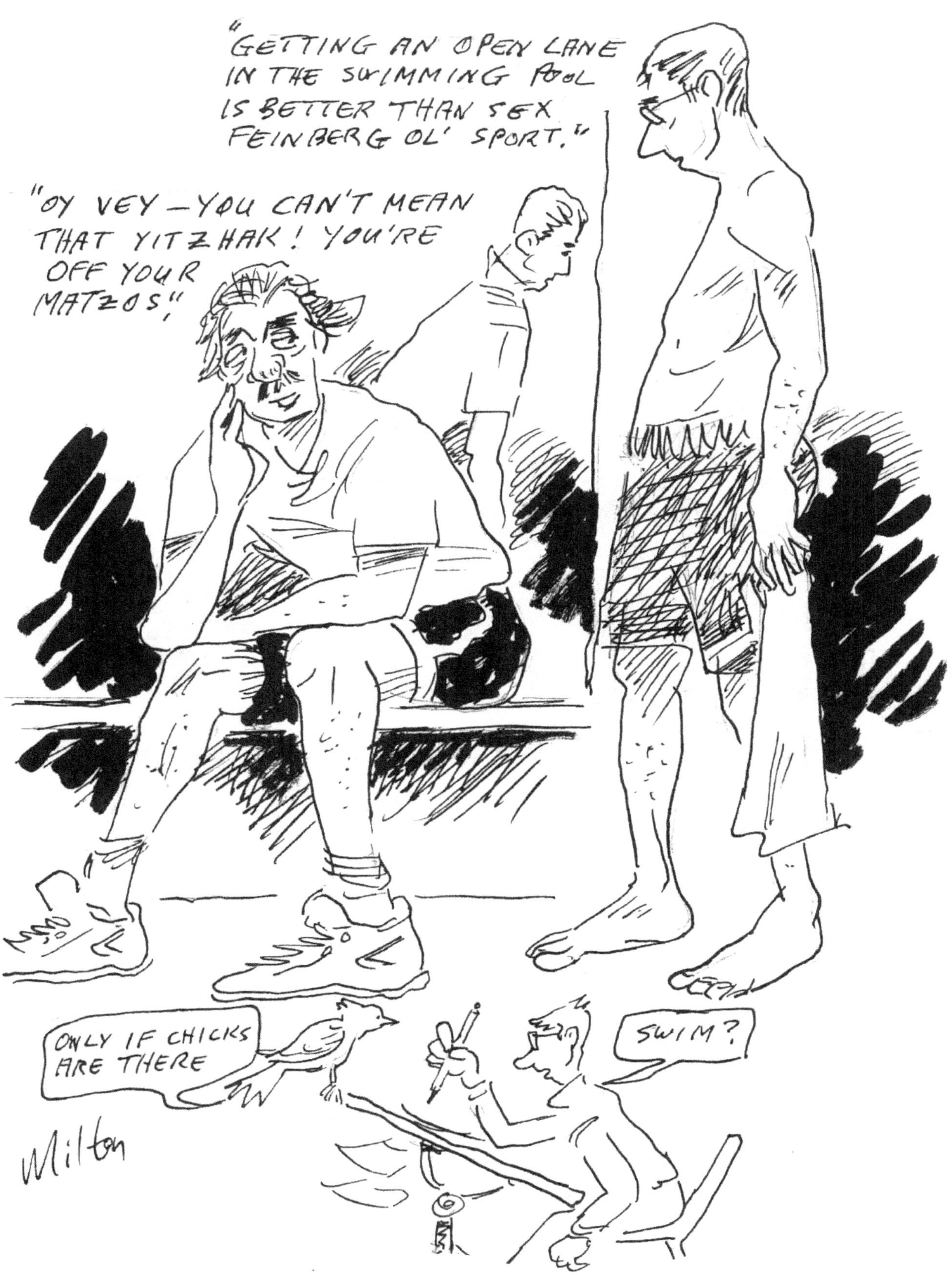
"GETTING AN OPEN LANE IN THE SWIMMING POOL IS BETTER THAN SEX FEINBERG OL' SPORT."
"OY VEY—YOU CAN'T MEAN THAT YITZHAK! YOU'RE OFF YOUR MATZOS!"
ONLY IF CHICKS ARE THERE
SWIM?
Milton

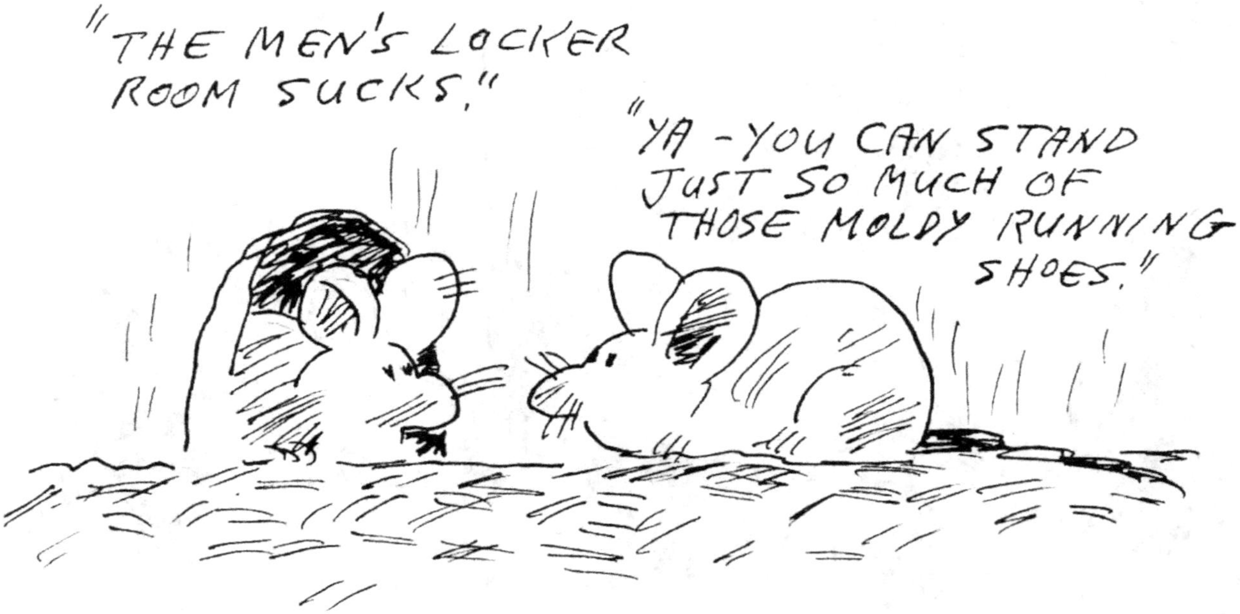
"THE MEN'S LOCKER ROOM SUCKS."
"YA - YOU CAN STAND JUST SO MUCH OF THOSE MOLDY RUNNING SHOES."

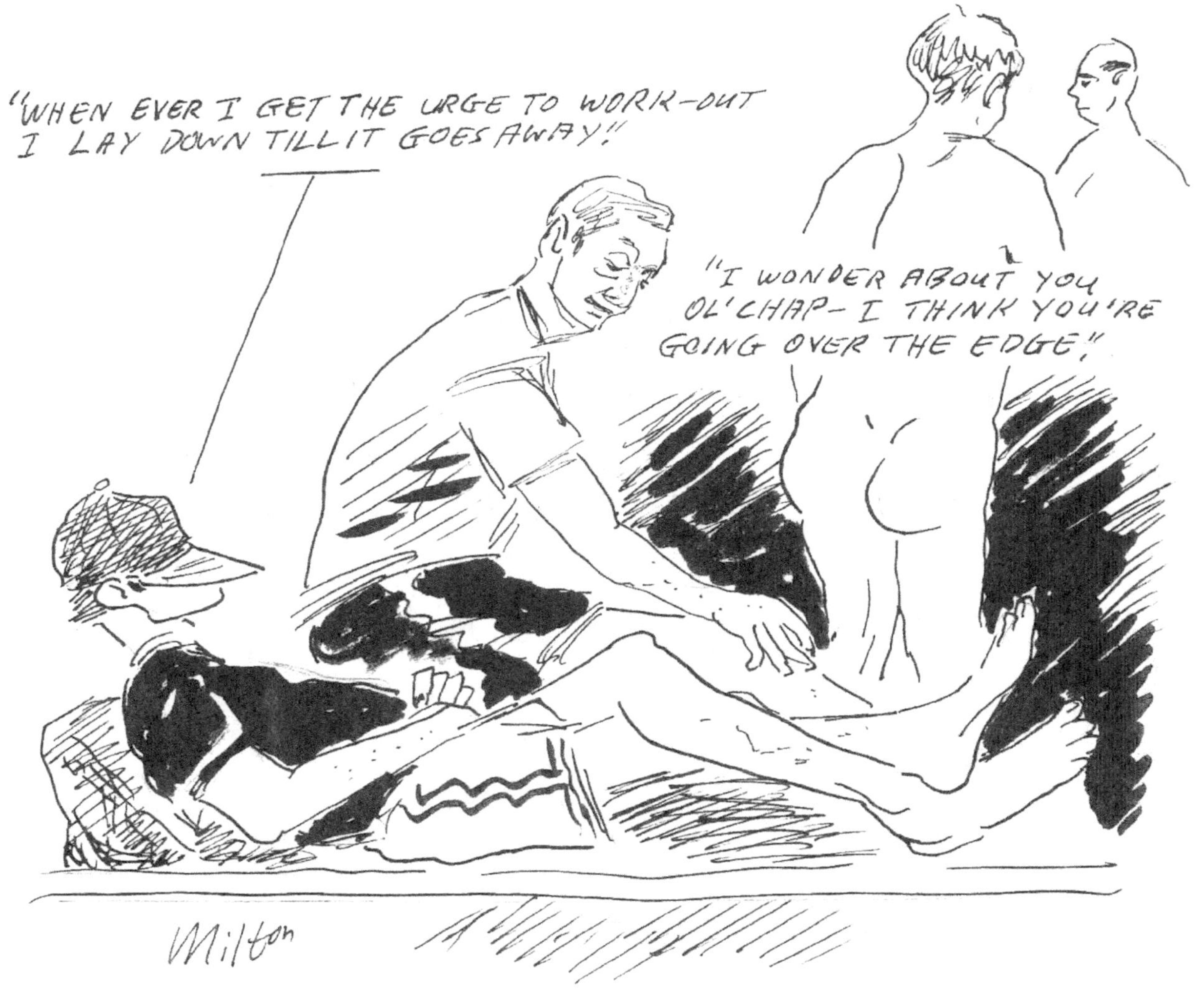
"WHEN EVER I GET THE URGE TO WORK-OUT I LAY DOWN TILL IT GOES AWAY!"
"I WONDER ABOUT YOU OL' CHAP- I THINK YOU'RE GOING OVER THE EDGE!"
Milton

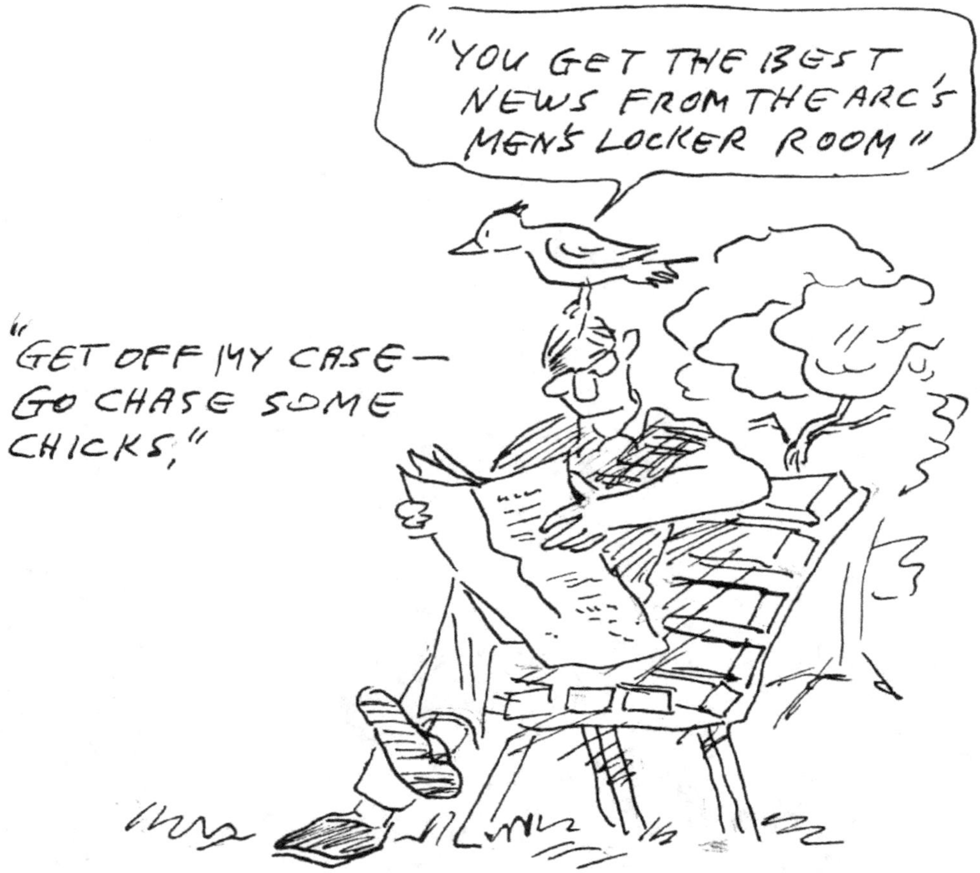
"YOU GET THE BEST NEWS FROM THE ARC's MEN'S LOCKER ROOM"
"GET OFF MY CASE— GO CHASE SOME CHICKS."

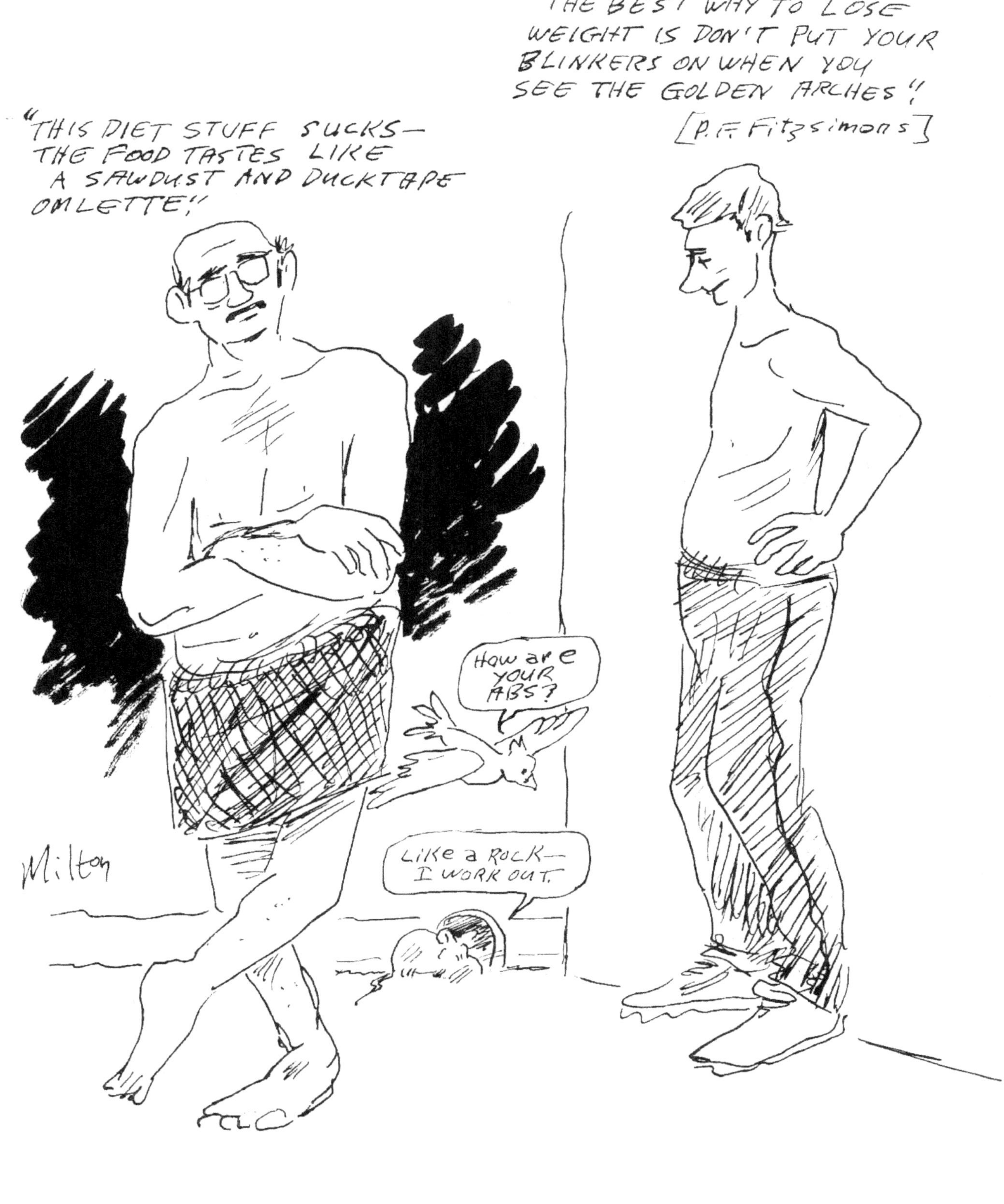
"THE BEST WAY TO LOSE WEIGHT IS DON'T PUT YOUR BLINKERS ON WHEN YOU SEE THE GOLDEN ARCHES!"
[P.F. Fitzsimons]
"THIS DIET STUFF SUCKS— THE FOOD TASTES LIKE A SAWDUST AND DUCKTAPE OMLETTE!"
How are YOUR ABS?
Like a ROCK— I WORK OUT.
Milton

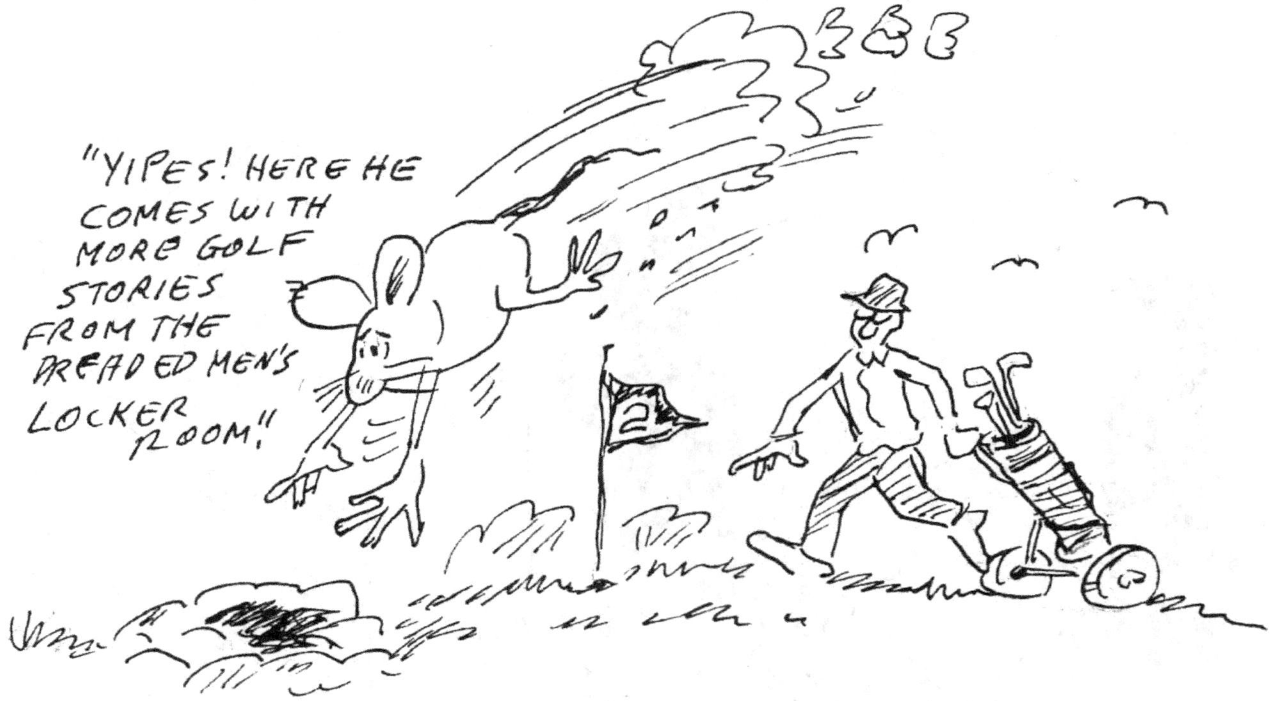
"YIPES! HERE HE COMES WITH MORE GOLF STORIES FROM THE DREADED MEN'S LOCKER ROOM!"
2

"SO WHAT YOU'RE SAYING IS WIN OR LOSE, YOU LOSE?"

"WHEN I HIT A GREAT GOLF SHOT NOBODY'S WATCHING – BUT WHEN I HIT A LOUSY SHOT EVERYONE'S THERE!"

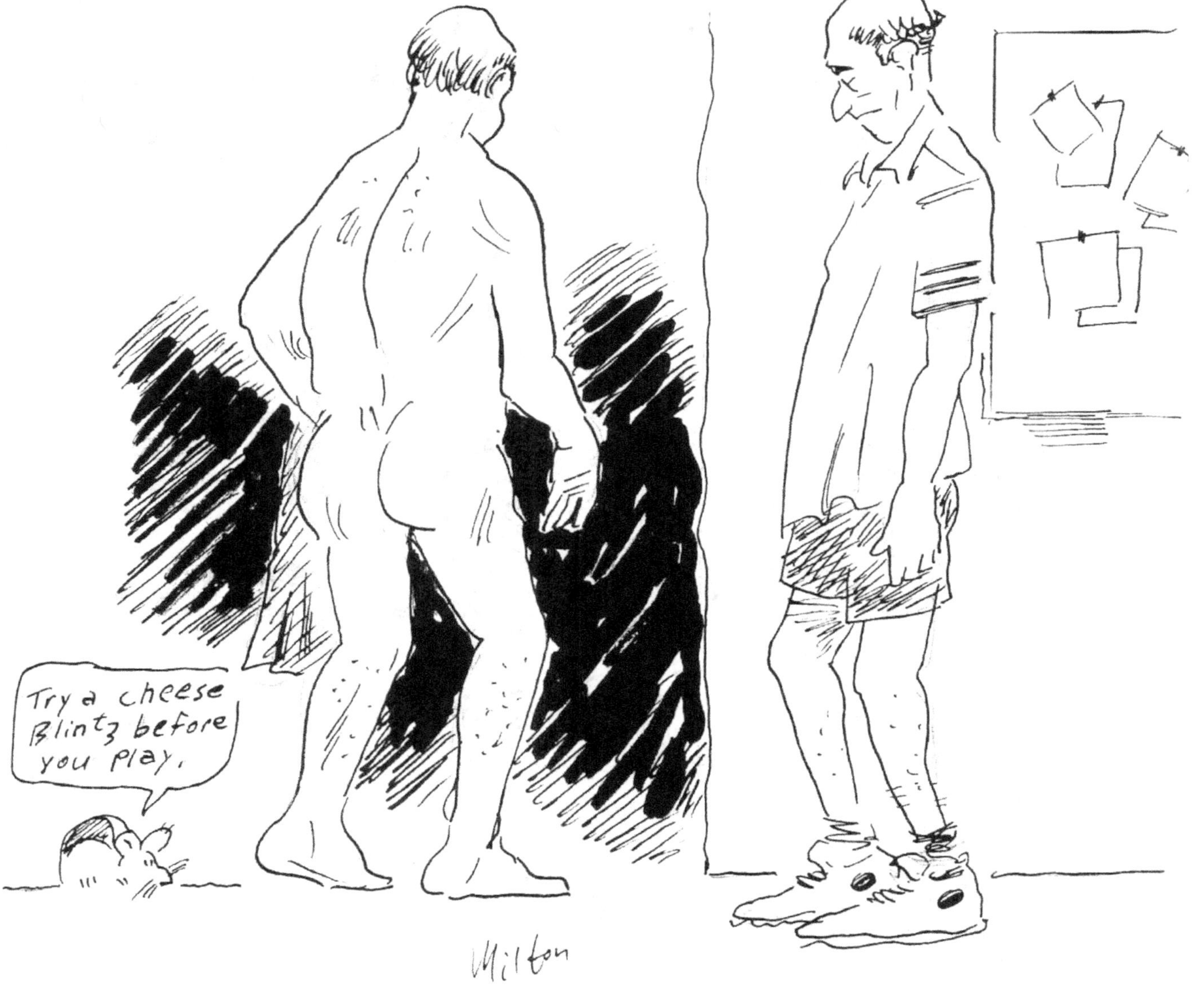
Try a cheese Blintz before you play.
Milton

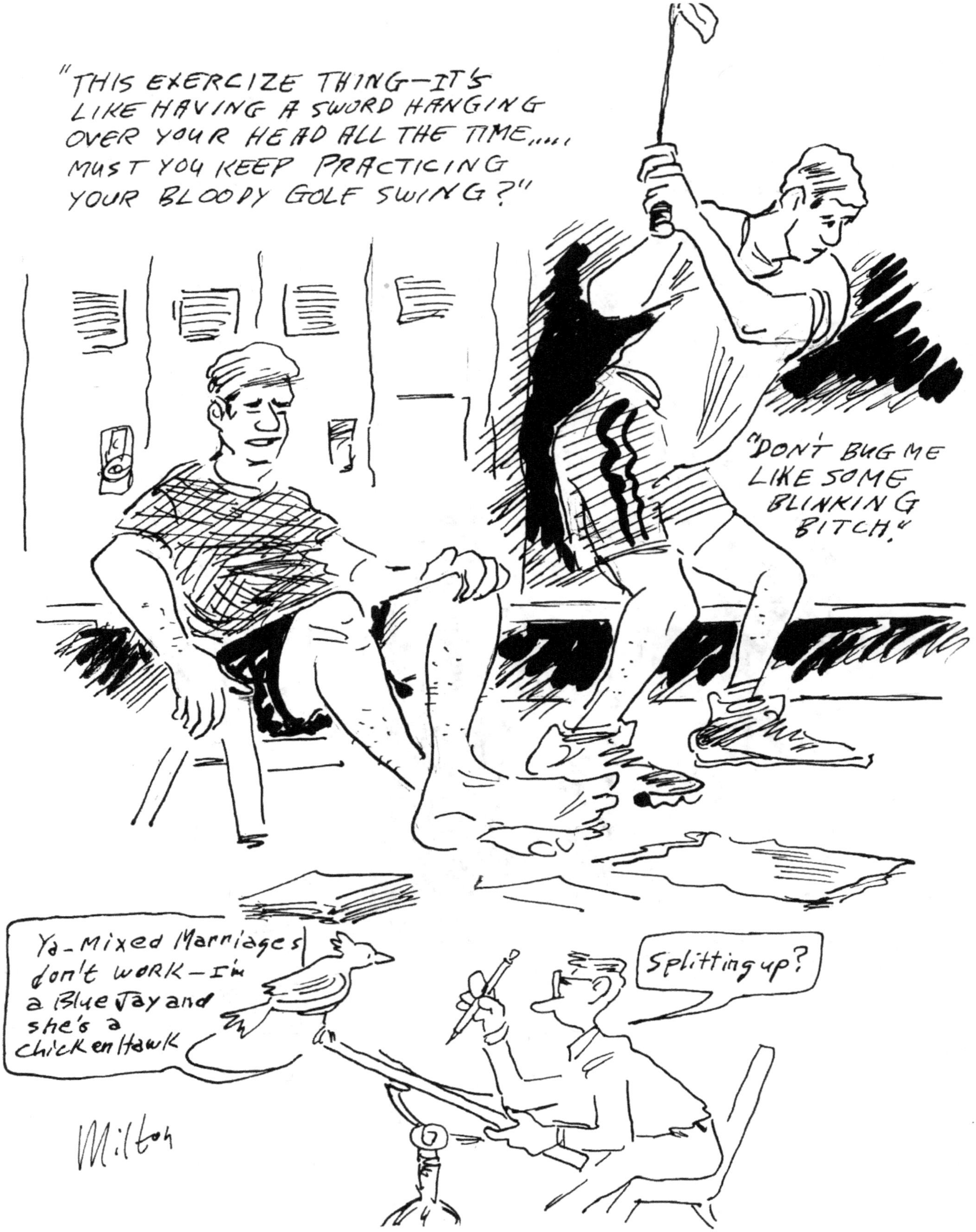
"THIS EXERCIZE THING—IT'S LIKE HAVING A SWORD HANGING OVER YOUR HEAD ALL THE TIME..... MUST YOU KEEP PRACTICING YOUR BLOODY GOLF SWING?"
"DON'T BUG ME LIKE SOME BLINKING BITCH."
Ya-Mixed Marriages don't work—I'm a Blue Jay and she's a chicken Hawk
Splitting up?
Milton

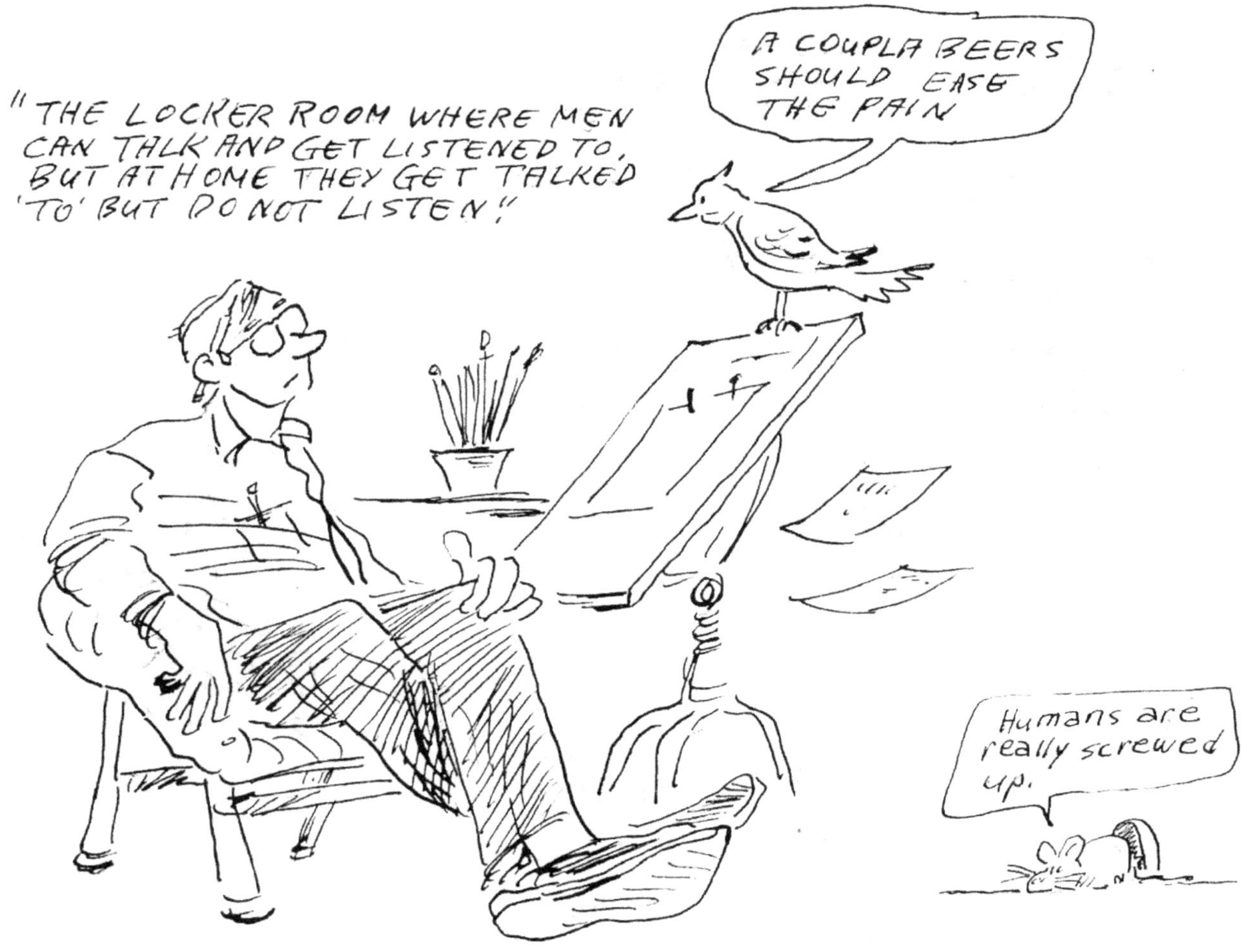
"THE LOCKER ROOM WHERE MEN CAN TALK AND GET LISTENED TO, BUT AT HOME THEY GET TALKED 'TO' BUT DO NOT LISTEN!"
A COUPLA BEERS SHOULD EASE THE PAIN
Humans are really screwed up.

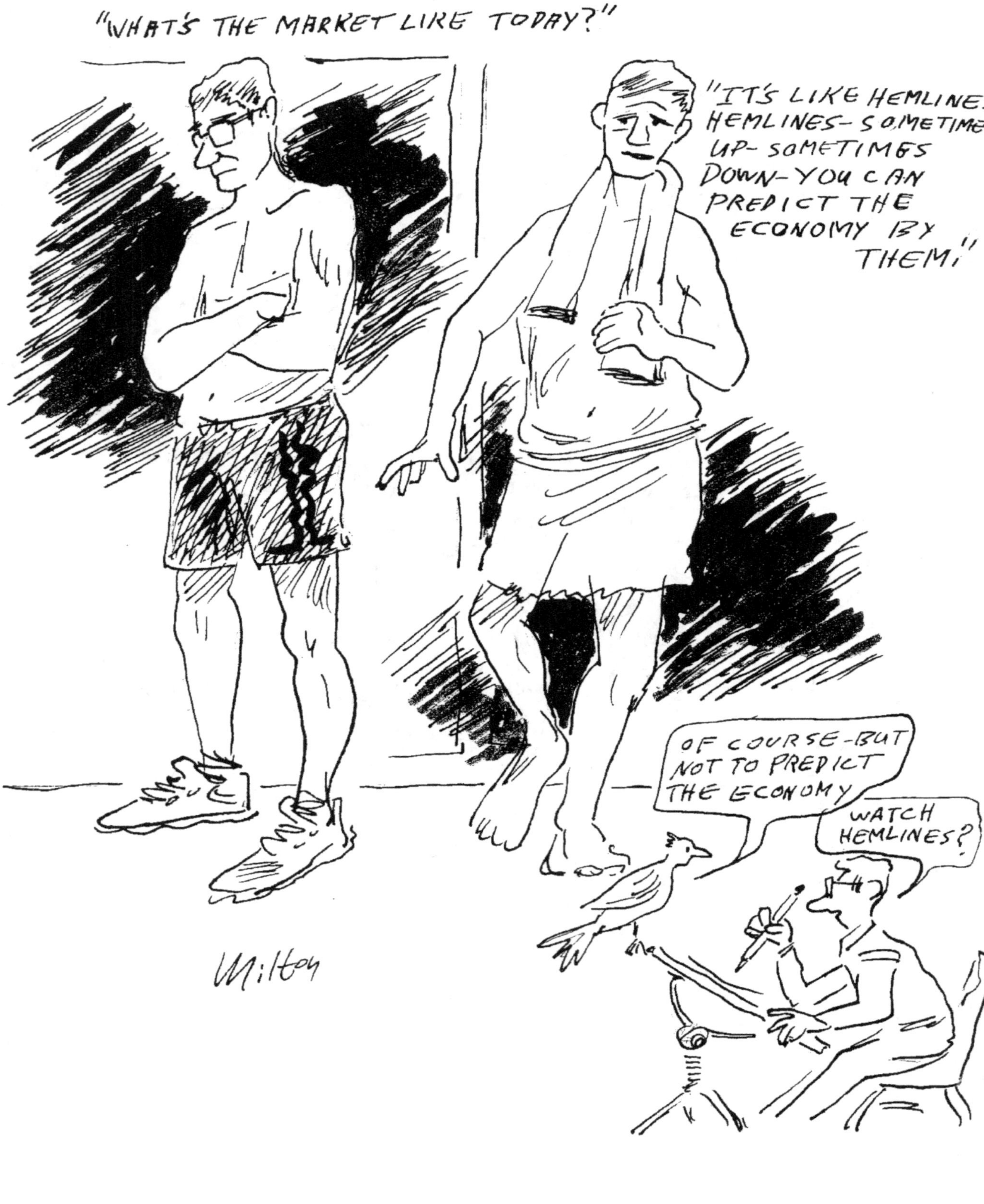
"WHAT'S THE MARKET LIKE TODAY?"
"IT'S LIKE HEMLINES. HEMLINES- SOMETIMES UP- SOMETIMES DOWN- YOU CAN PREDICT THE ECONOMY BY THEM."
OF COURSE-BUT NOT TO PREDICT THE ECONOMY
WATCH HEMLINES?
Milton

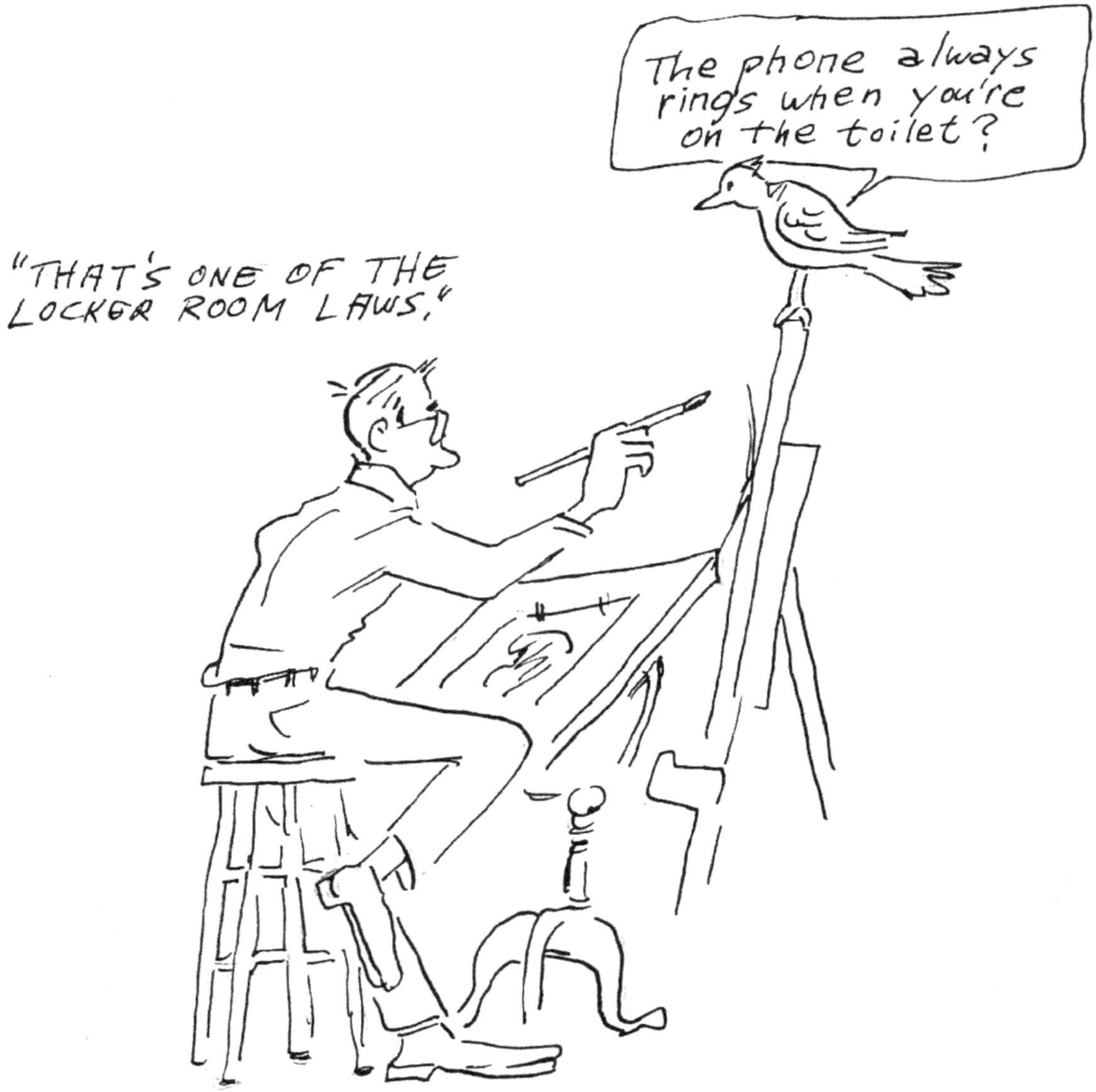

The phone always rings when you're on the toilet?
"THAT'S ONE OF THE LOCKER ROOM LAWS."

"WHY IS IT IF YOU ASK A WOMAN IF SHE WOULD RATHER CATCH A FLY BALL OR RESCUE A BABY—SHE WILL CHOOSE THE BABY WITHOUT EVEN ASKING IF THERE'S MEN ON BASE."

[Dave Barry]

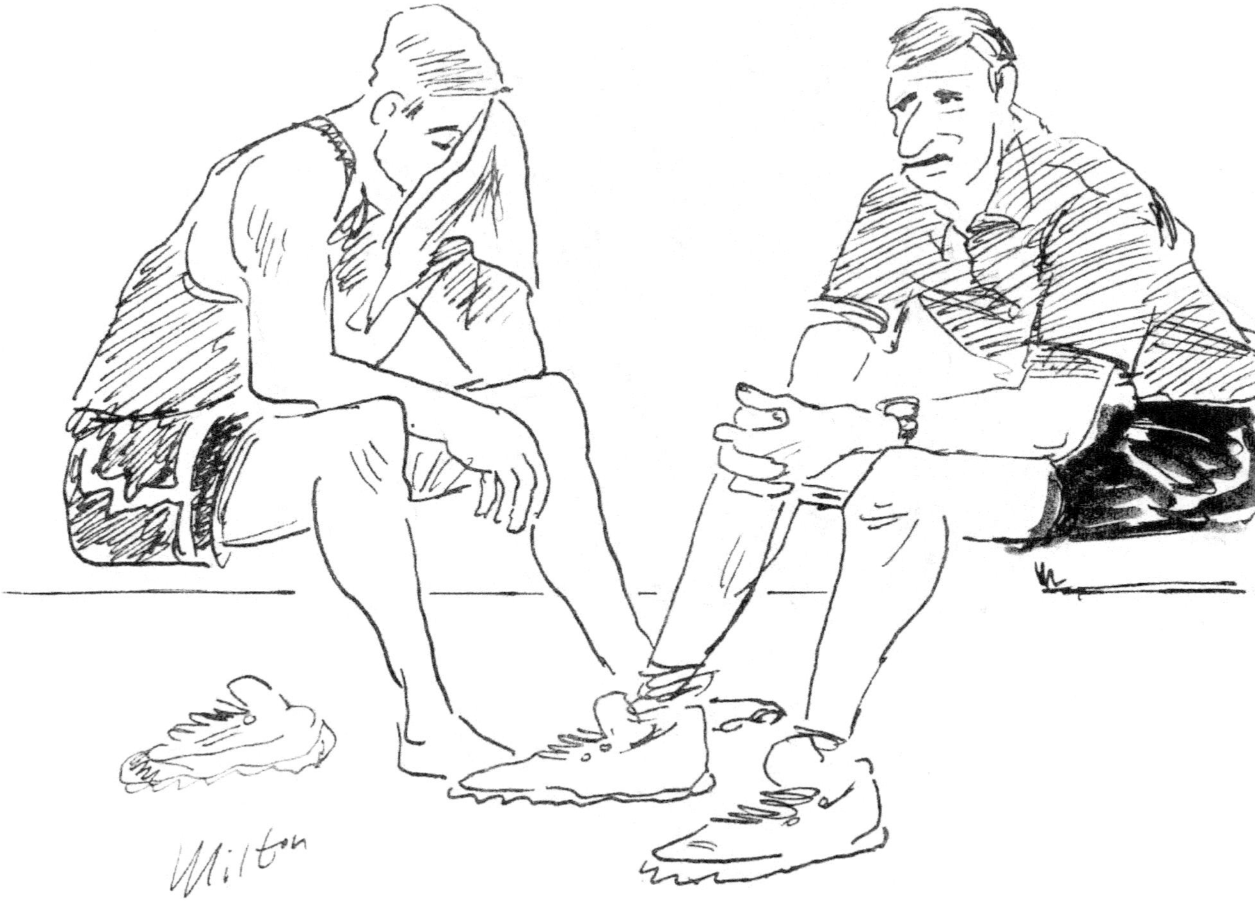
Milton

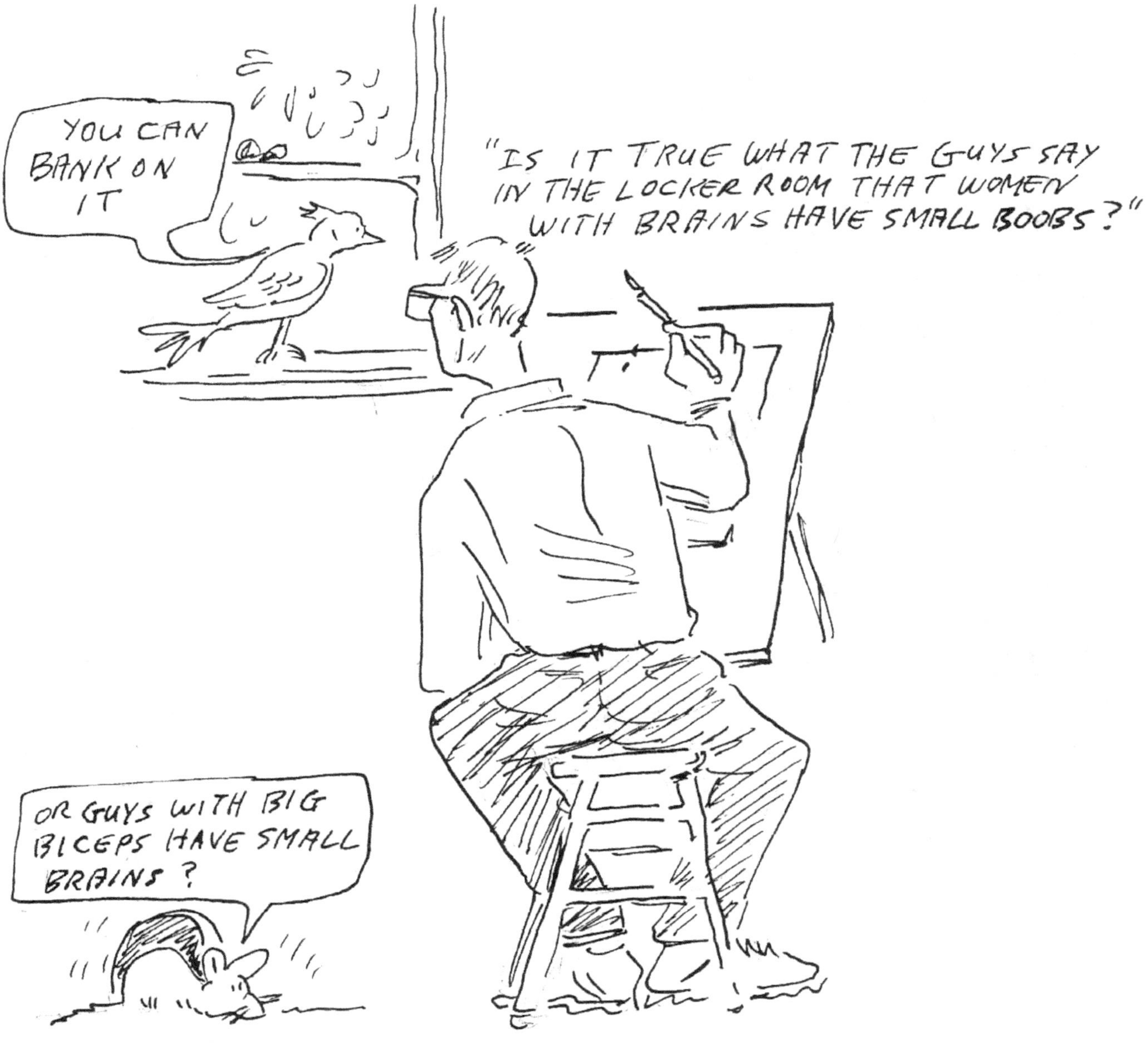
YOU CAN BANK ON IT
"IS IT TRUE WHAT THE GUYS SAY IN THE LOCKER ROOM THAT WOMEN WITH BRAINS HAVE SMALL BOOBS?"
OR GUYS WITH BIG BICEPS HAVE SMALL BRAINS ?

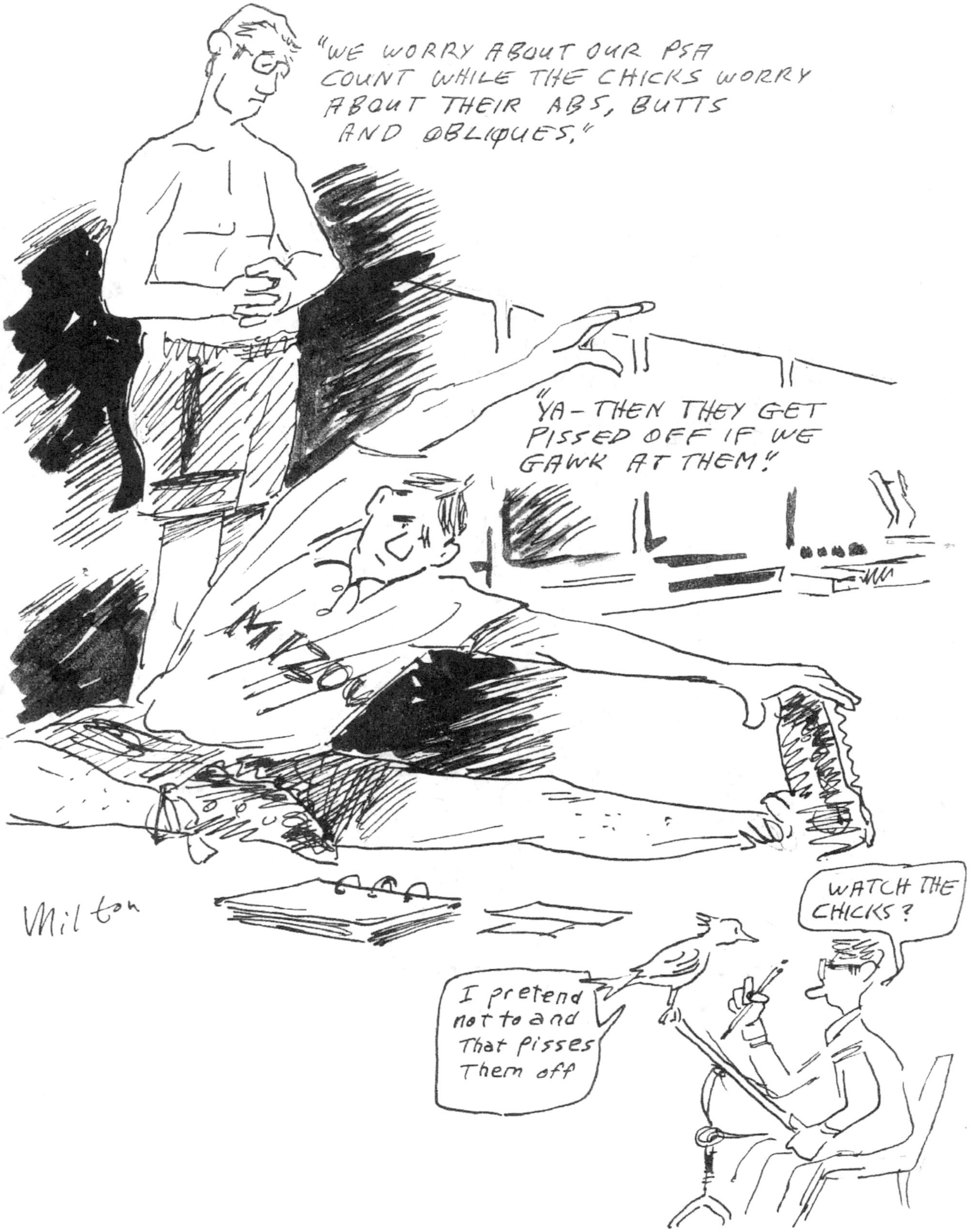
"WE WORRY ABOUT OUR PSA COUNT WHILE THE CHICKS WORRY ABOUT THEIR ABS, BUTTS AND OBLIQUES."
"YA-THEN THEY GET PISSED OFF IF WE GAWK AT THEM!"
Milton
WATCH THE CHICKS?
I pretend not to and That pisses Them off

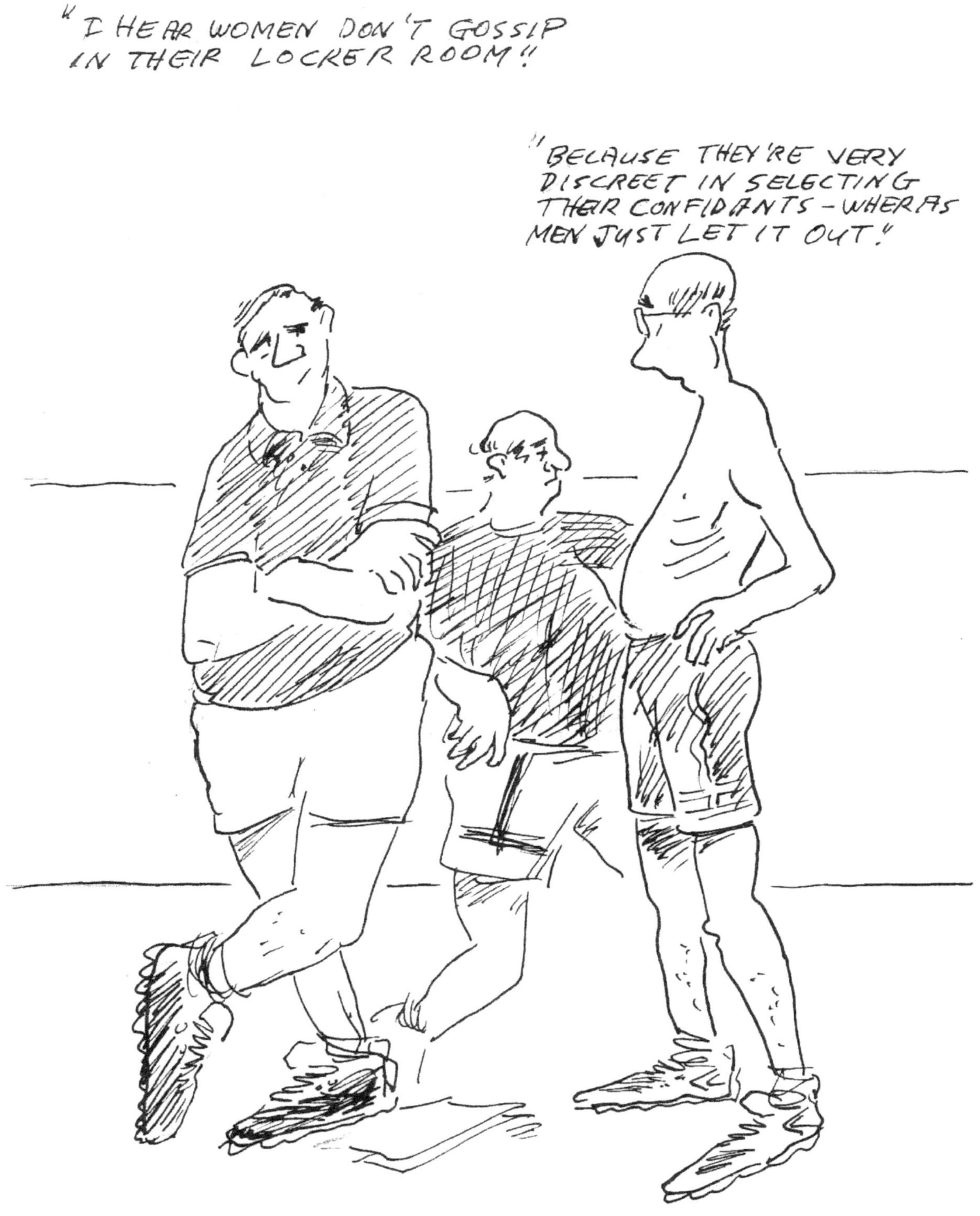
"I HEAR WOMEN DON'T GOSSIP IN THEIR LOCKER ROOM!"
"BECAUSE THEY'RE VERY DISCREET IN SELECTING THEIR CONFIDANTS - WHERAS MEN JUST LET IT OUT!"

"THE GUYS IN THE LOCKER ROOM ALL GO FOR THE YOUNG CHICKS."

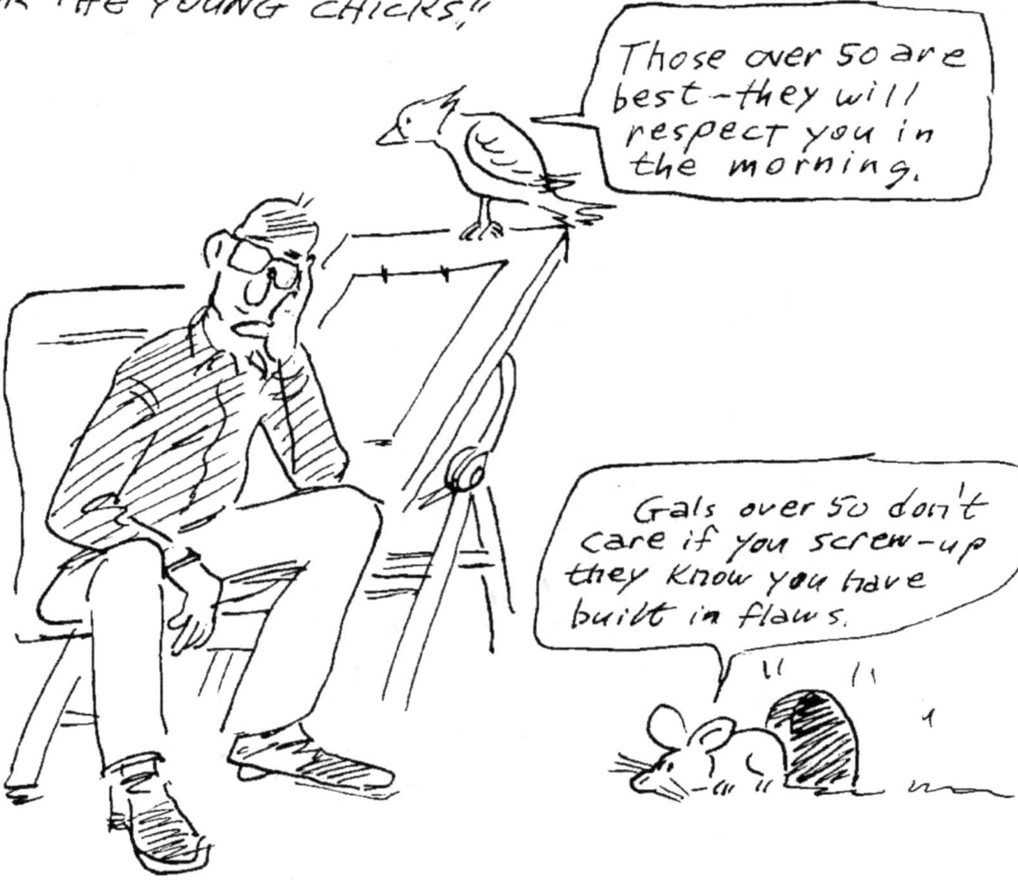
Those over 50 are best - they will respect you in the morning.
Gals over 50 don't care if you screw-up they know you have built in flaws.

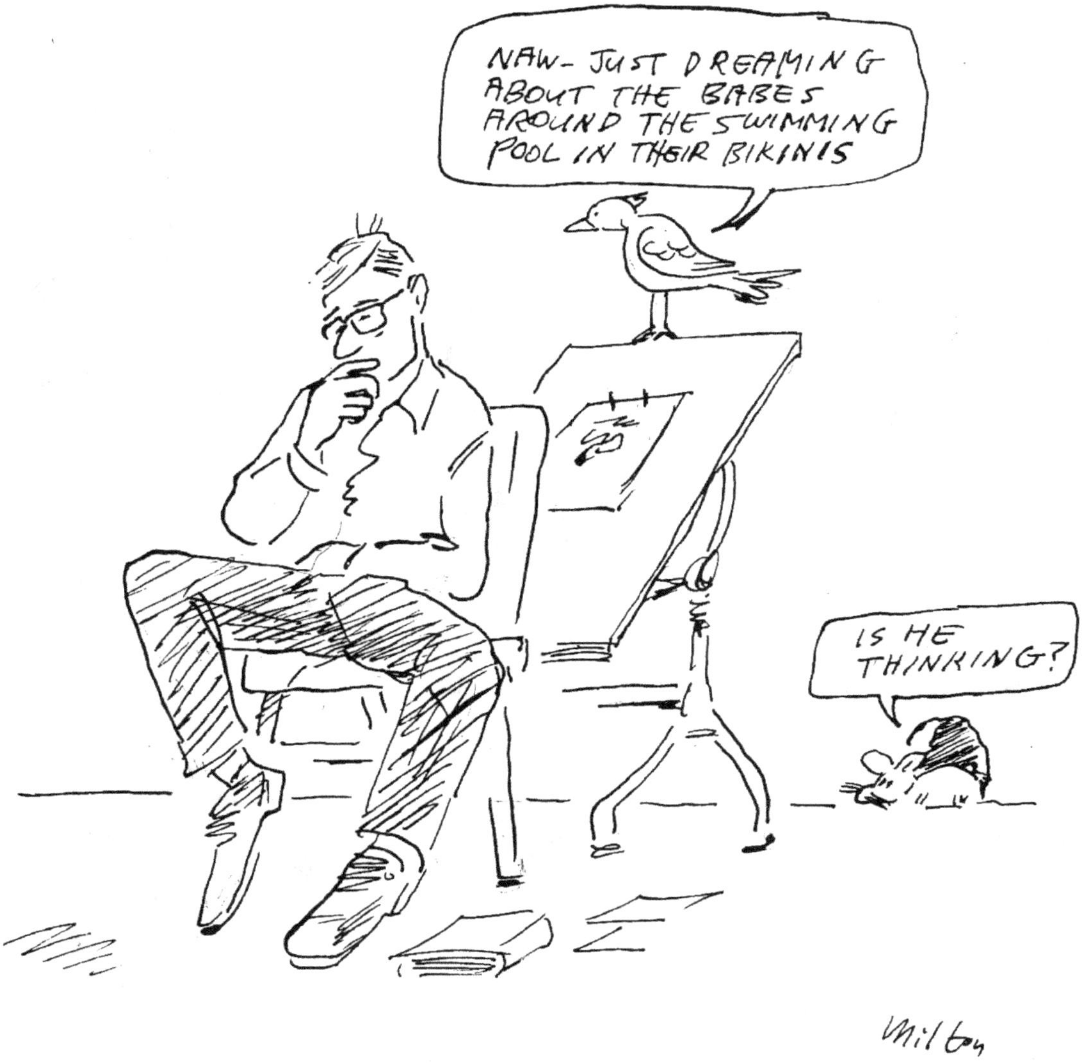
NAW- JUST DREAMING ABOUT THE BABES AROUND THE SWIMMING POOL IN THEIR BIKINIS
IS HE THINKING?
Milton

"BUS TOURS– OLD BAGS TALK ABOUT THEIR LAST OPERATION AND OLD GEEZERS TELL GOLF AND WAR STORIES.... IT ALL SUCKS!"

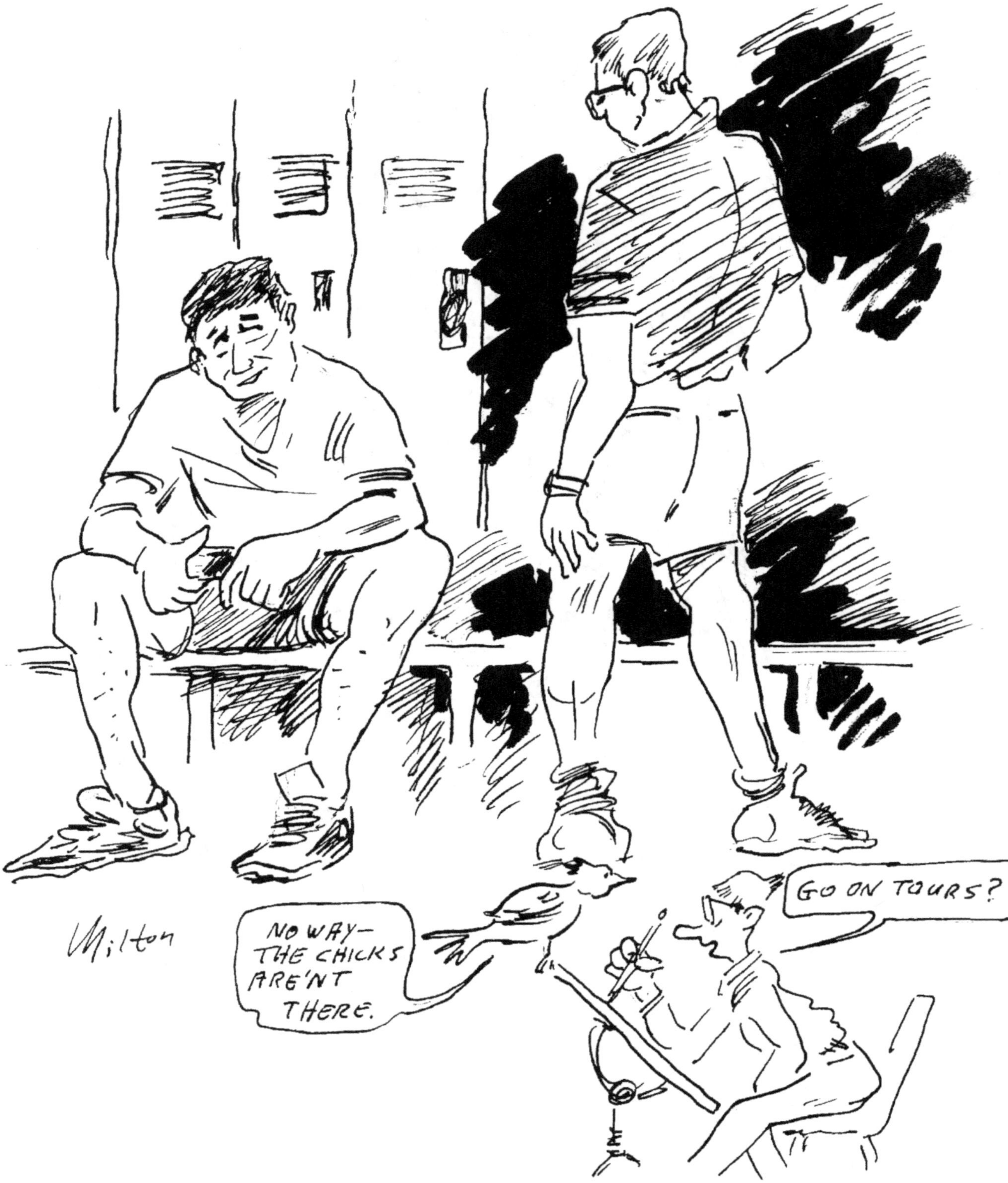
Milton
GO ON TOURS?
NO WAY– THE CHICKS AREN'T THERE.

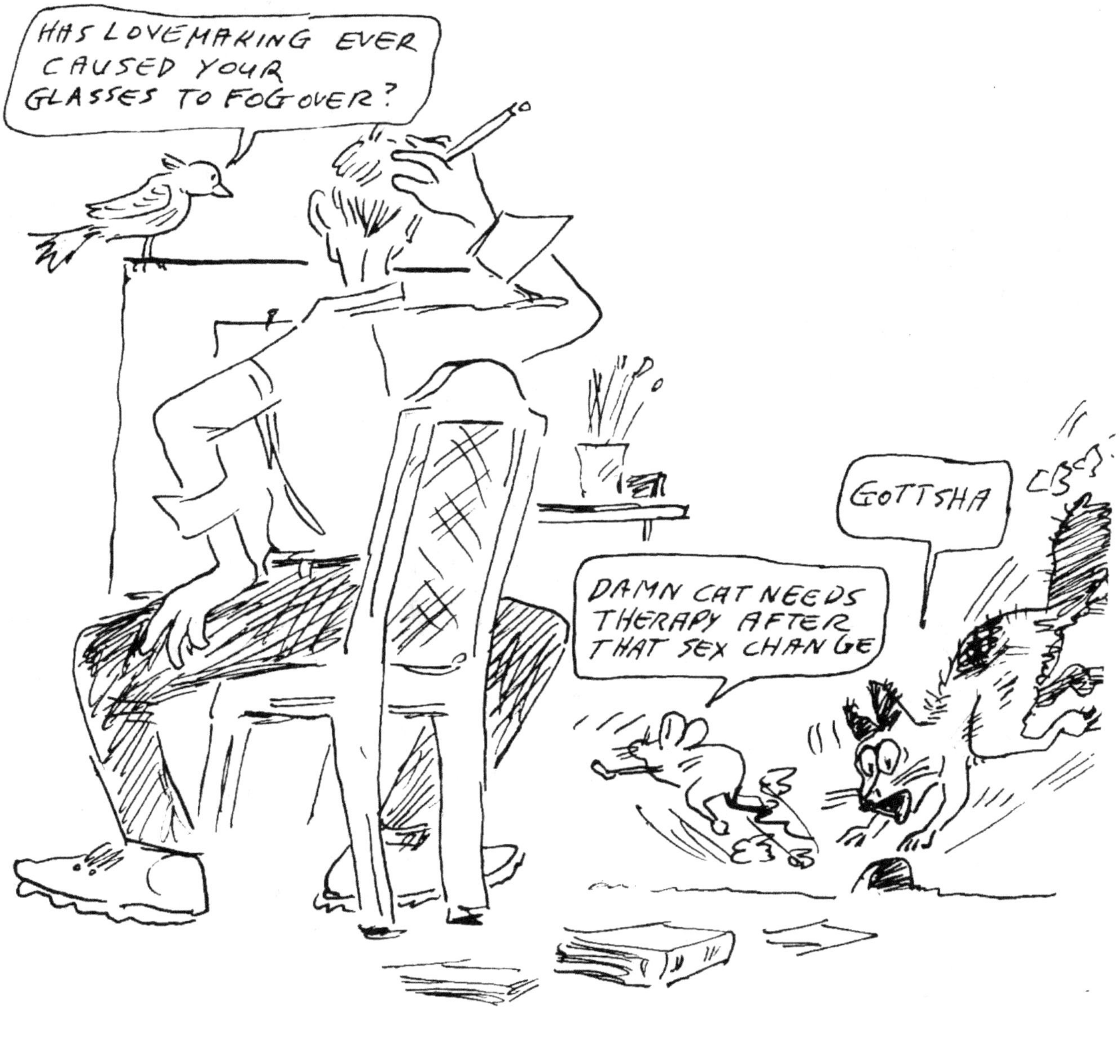
HAS LOVEMAKING EVER CAUSED YOUR GLASSES TO FOG OVER?
DAMN CAT NEEDS THERAPY AFTER THAT SEX CHANGE
GOTTSHA

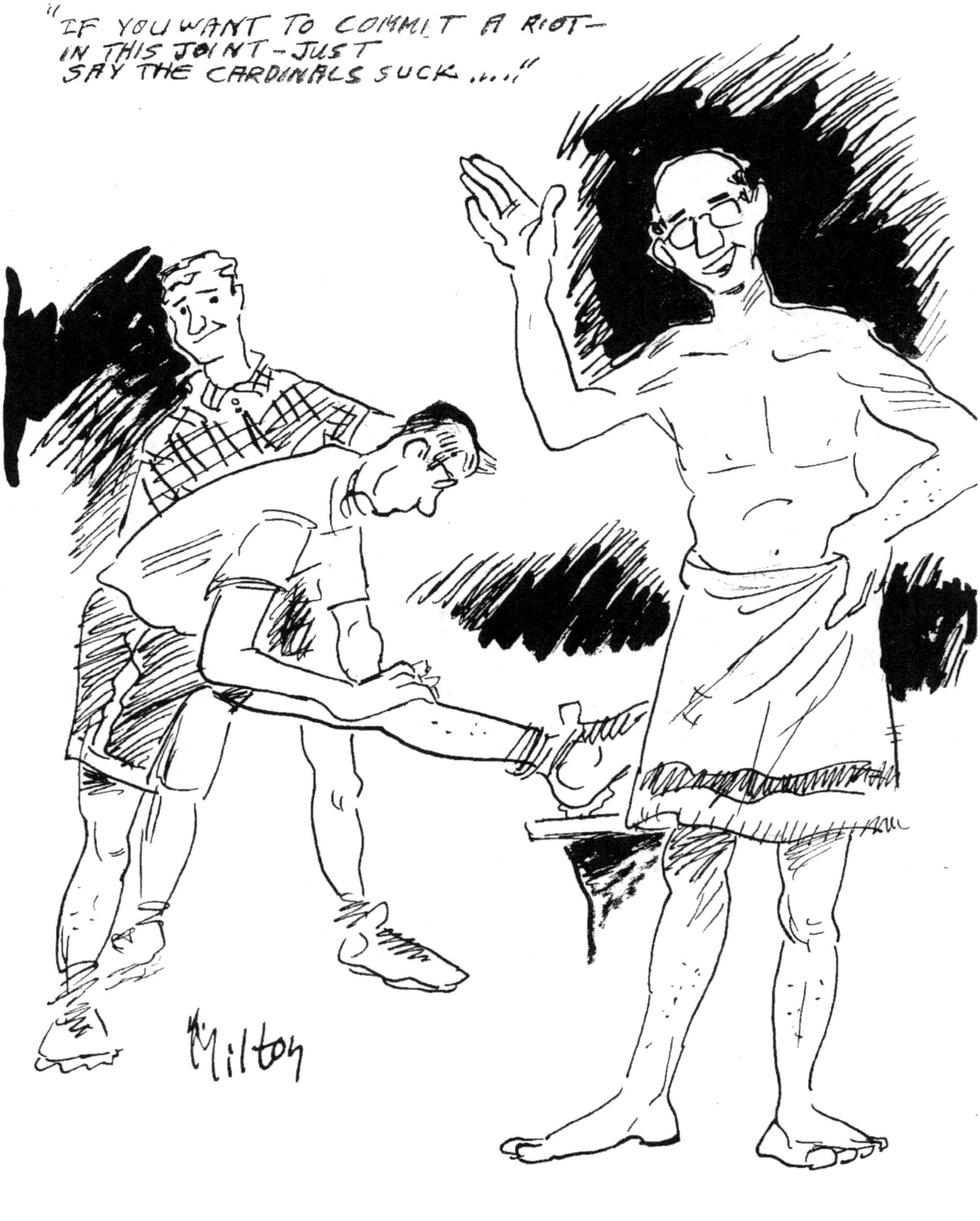
"IF YOU WANT TO COMMIT A RIOT–
IN THIS JOINT–JUST
SAY THE CARDINALS SUCK....."
Milton

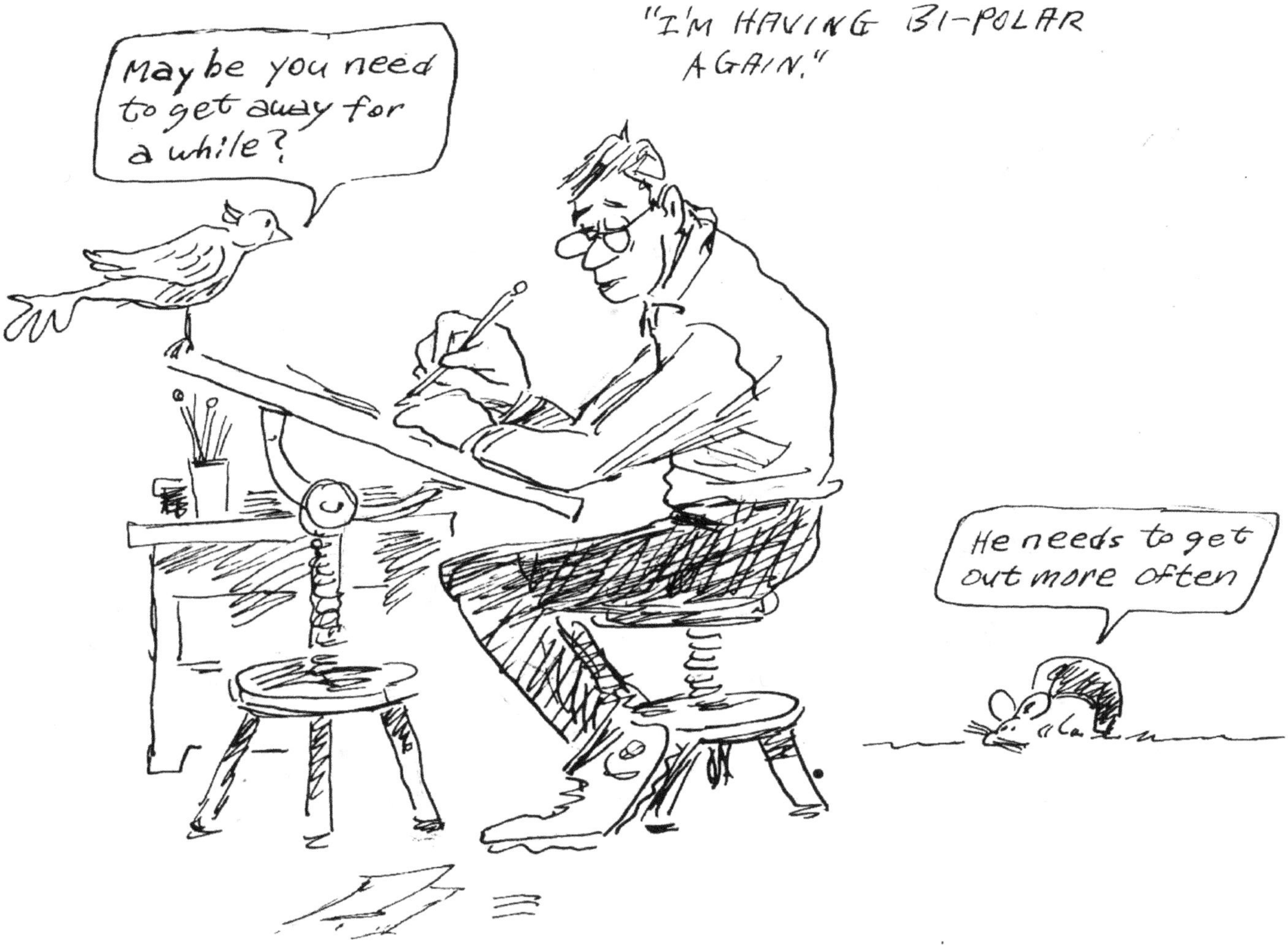
Maybe you need to get away for a while?
"I'M HAVING BI-POLAR AGAIN."
He needs to get out more often

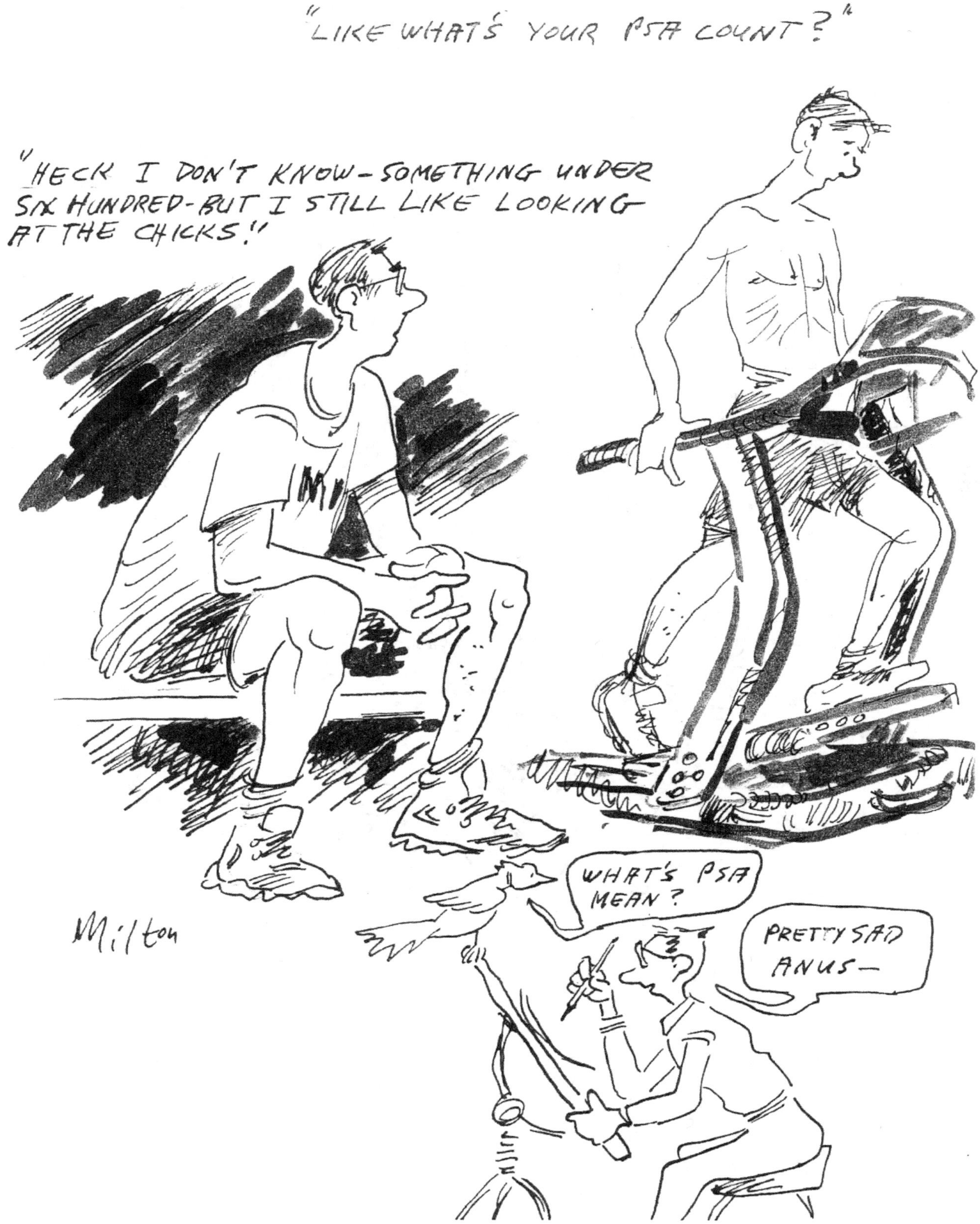
"LIKE WHAT'S YOUR PSA COUNT?"
"HECK I DON'T KNOW - SOMETHING UNDER SIX HUNDRED - BUT I STILL LIKE LOOKING AT THE CHICKS!"
Milton
WHAT'S PSA MEAN?
PRETTY SAD ANUS -

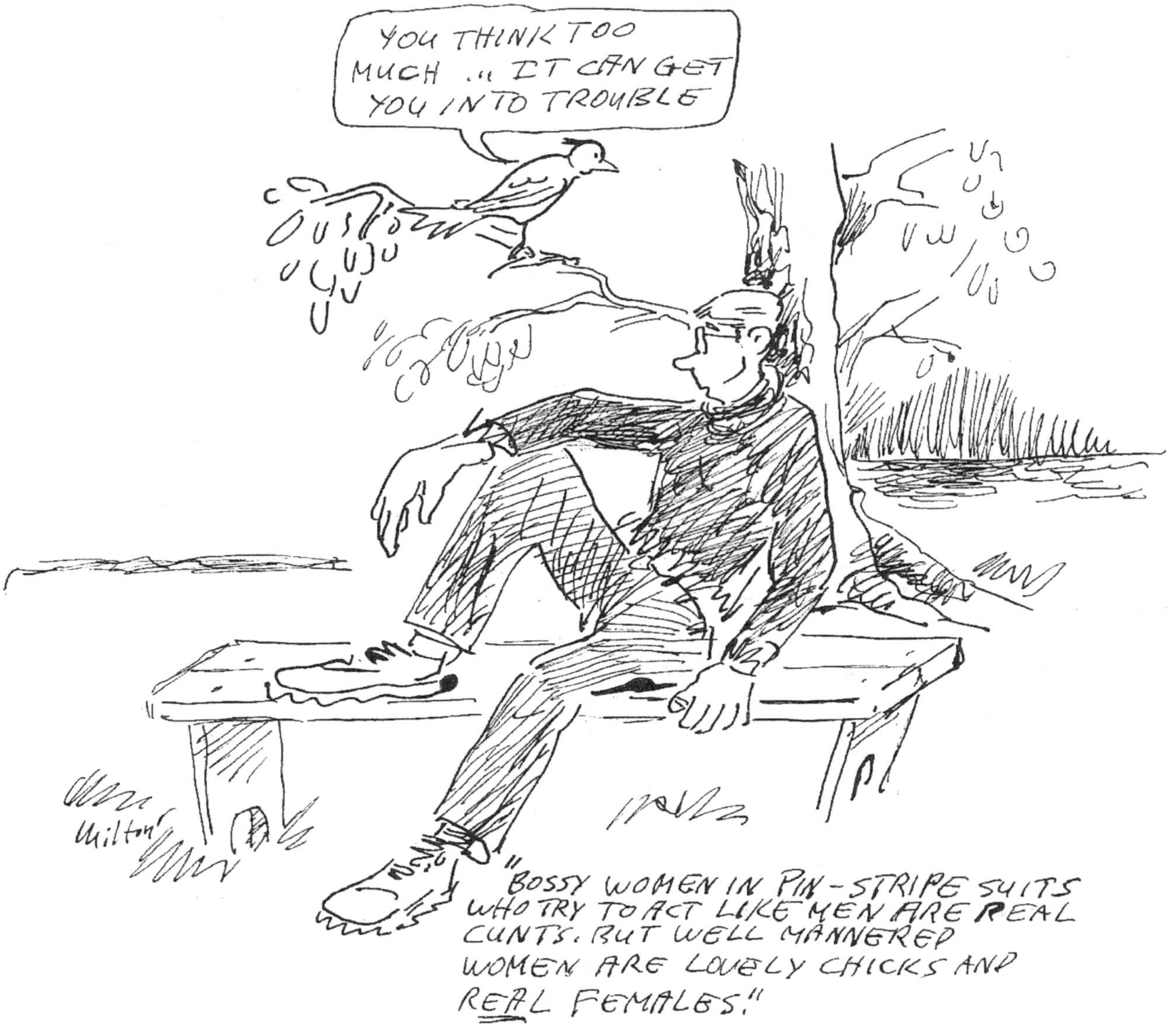
YOU THINK TOO MUCH .. IT CAN GET YOU INTO TROUBLE
Milton
"BOSSY WOMEN IN PIN-STRIPE SUITS WHO TRY TO ACT LIKE MEN ARE REAL CUNTS. BUT WELL MANNERED WOMEN ARE LOVELY CHICKS AND REAL FEMALES."

"BEHOLD OUR FRIEND MAYNARD'S FIRST NIGHT AS A NEWLYWED WAS A DISASTER - SHE COMPLAINED ABOUT HIS KEEPING HIS SHOES ON DURING SEX AND HE CHEWED GUM."

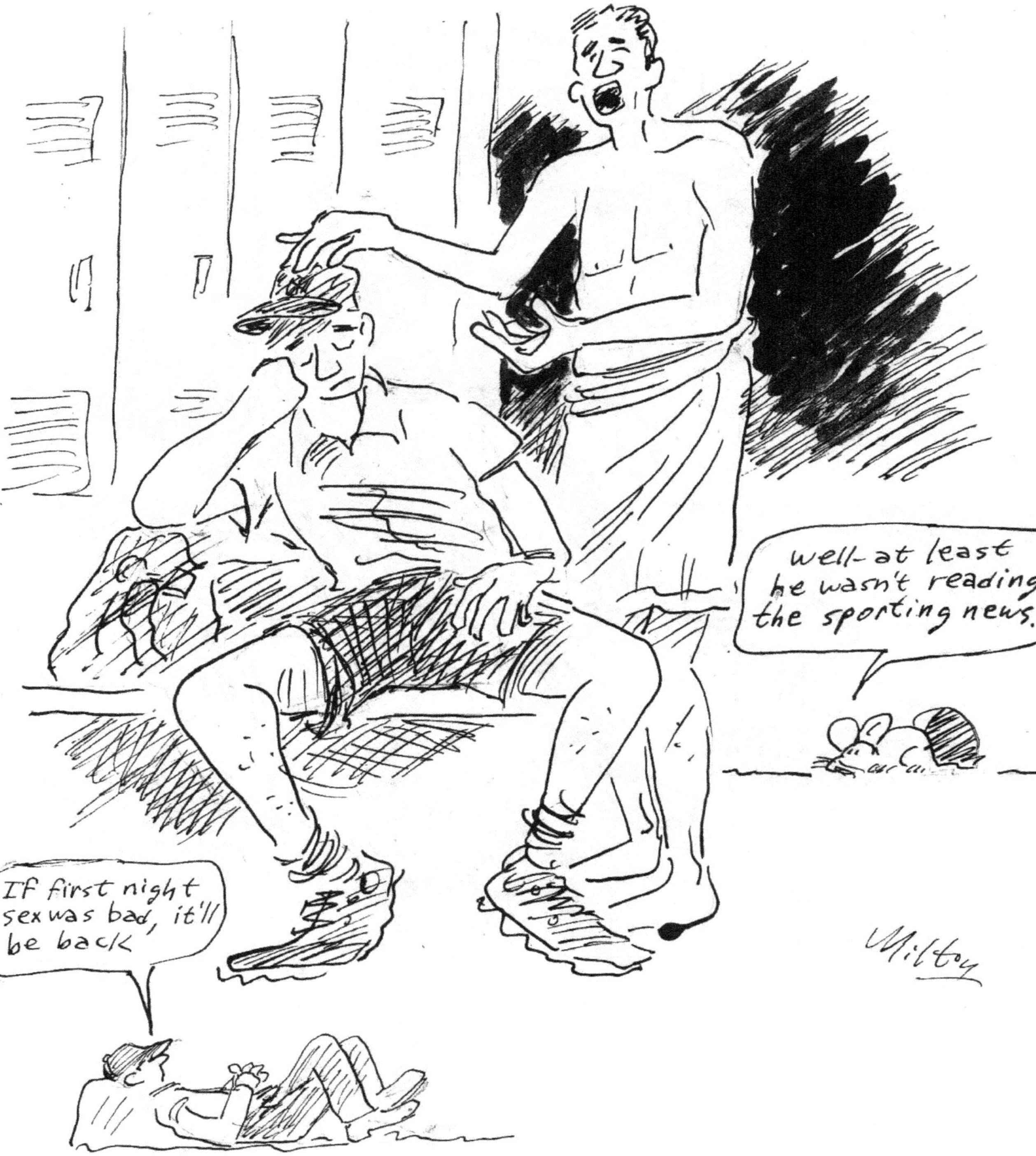

well-at least he wasn't reading the sporting news.
If first night sex was bad, it'll be back
Milton

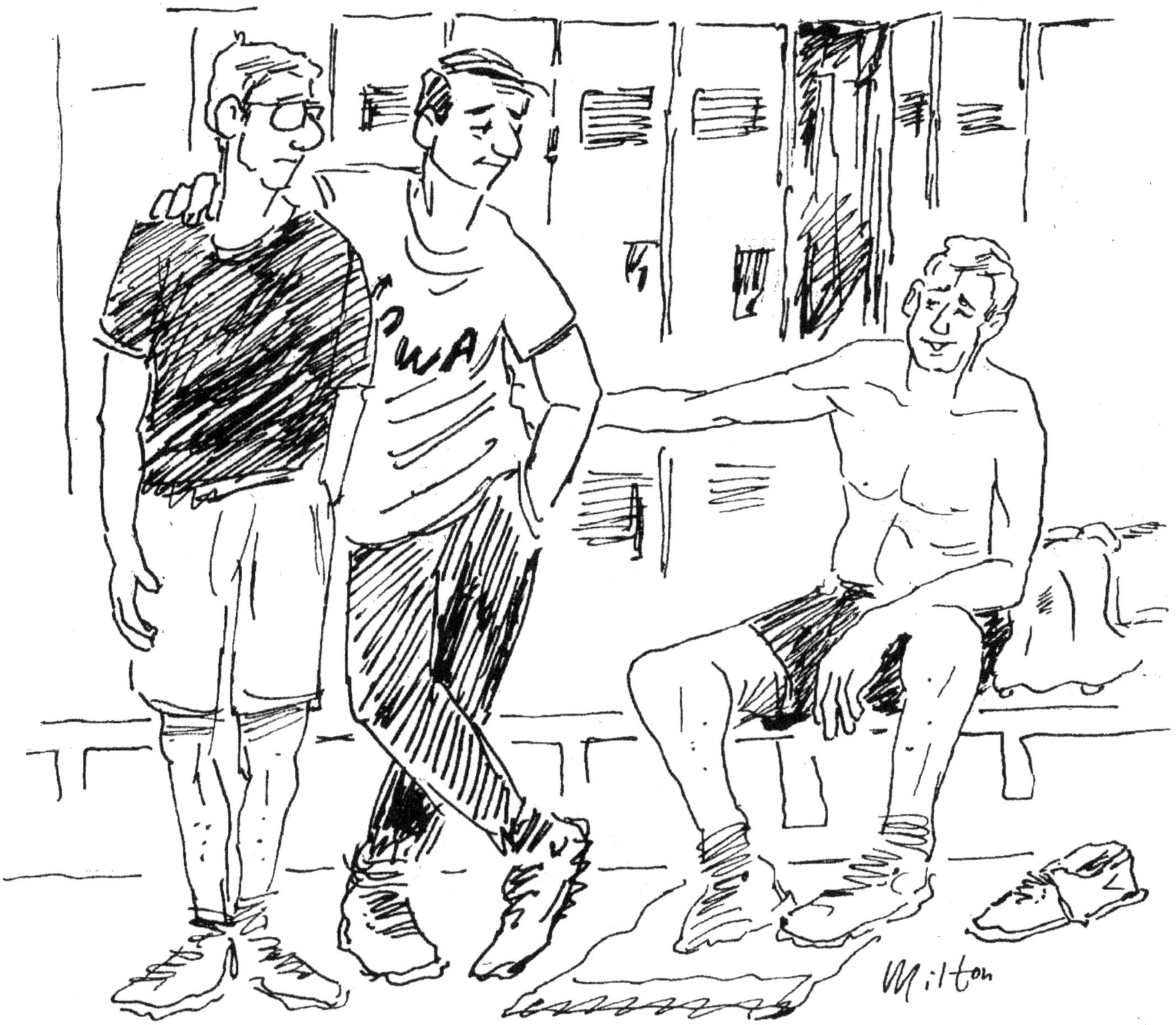
Milton

"LET'S GO TO A COWBOY BAR TONIGHT, I'M CELEBRATING TWENTY YEARS OF BEING DIVORCED!"

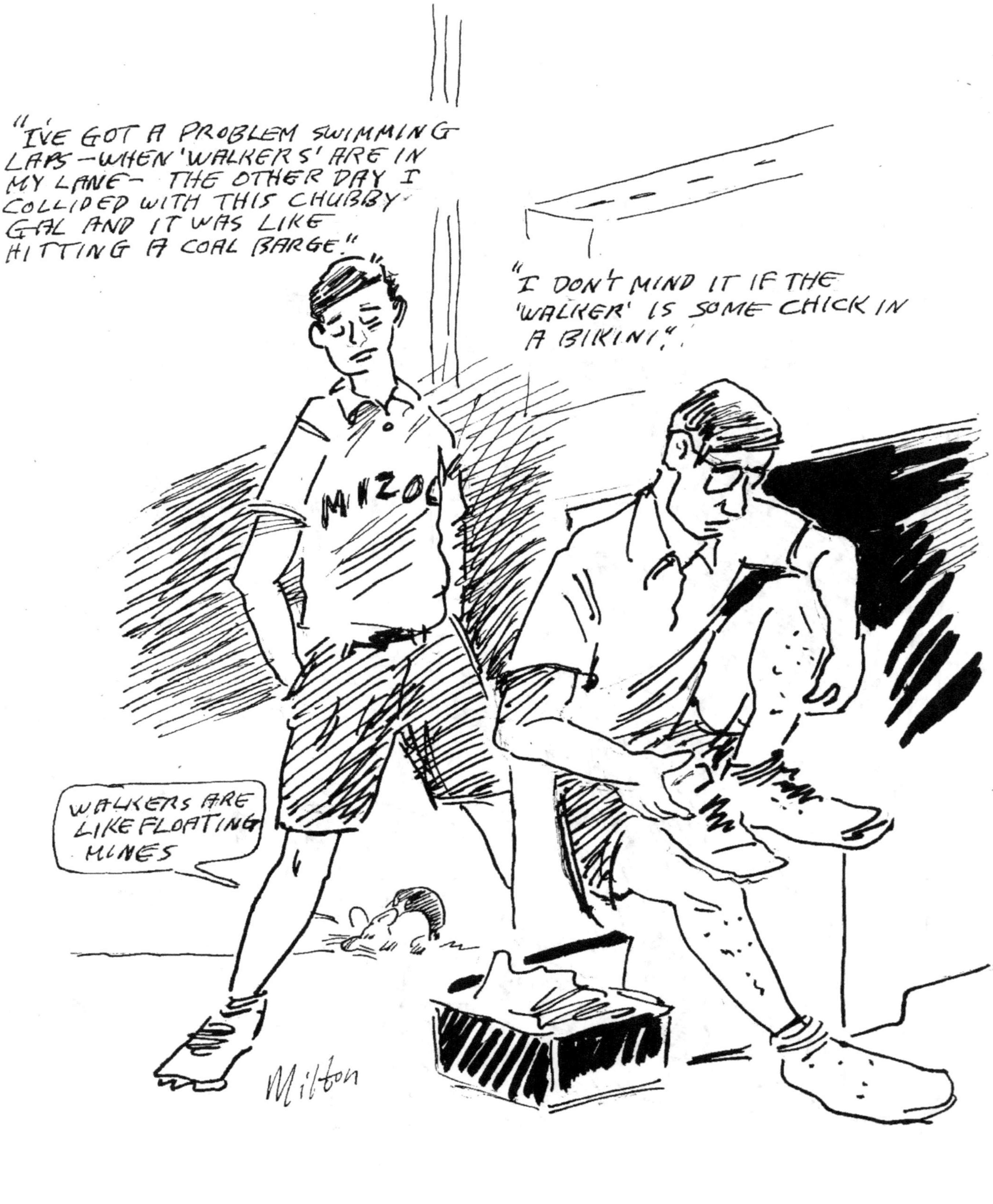
"I'VE GOT A PROBLEM SWIMMING LAPS—WHEN 'WALKERS' ARE IN MY LANE— THE OTHER DAY I COLLIDED WITH THIS CHUBBY GAL AND IT WAS LIKE HITTING A COAL BARGE."
"I DON'T MIND IT IF THE 'WALKER' IS SOME CHICK IN A BIKINI."
WALKERS ARE LIKE FLOATING MINES
MIZOU
Milton

THE LOCKER ROOM – FAVORITE HAUNT FOR BASEBALL TRIVIA FREAKS....

REMEMBER WHO DOUG GWOSDZ WAS?
"THAT'S EASY – SAN DIEGO CATCHER – NICKNAMED 'EYECHART' – PLAYED ABOUT SIX YEARS I THINK – FROM 1968–1974 OR SO!"
Milton

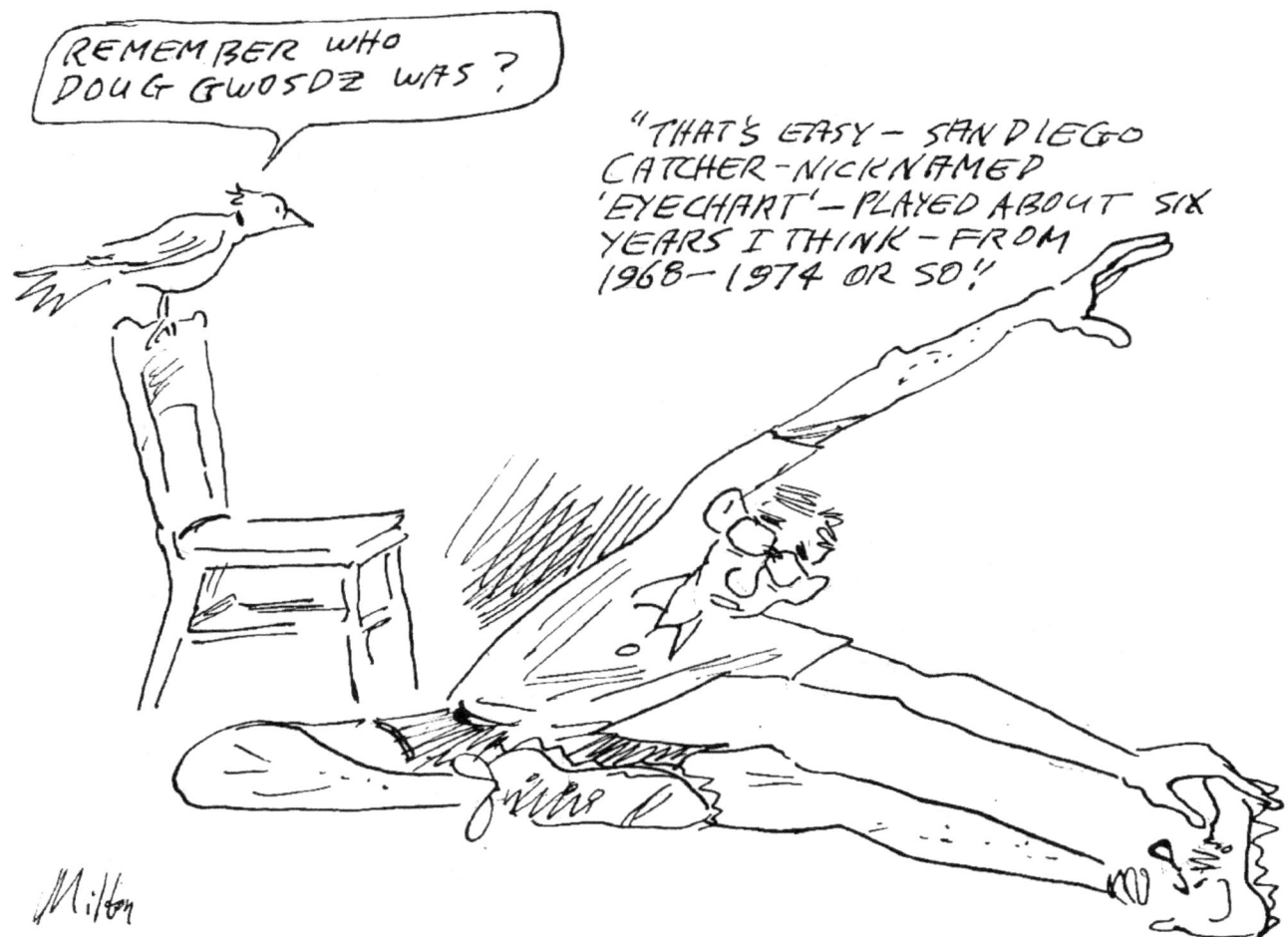

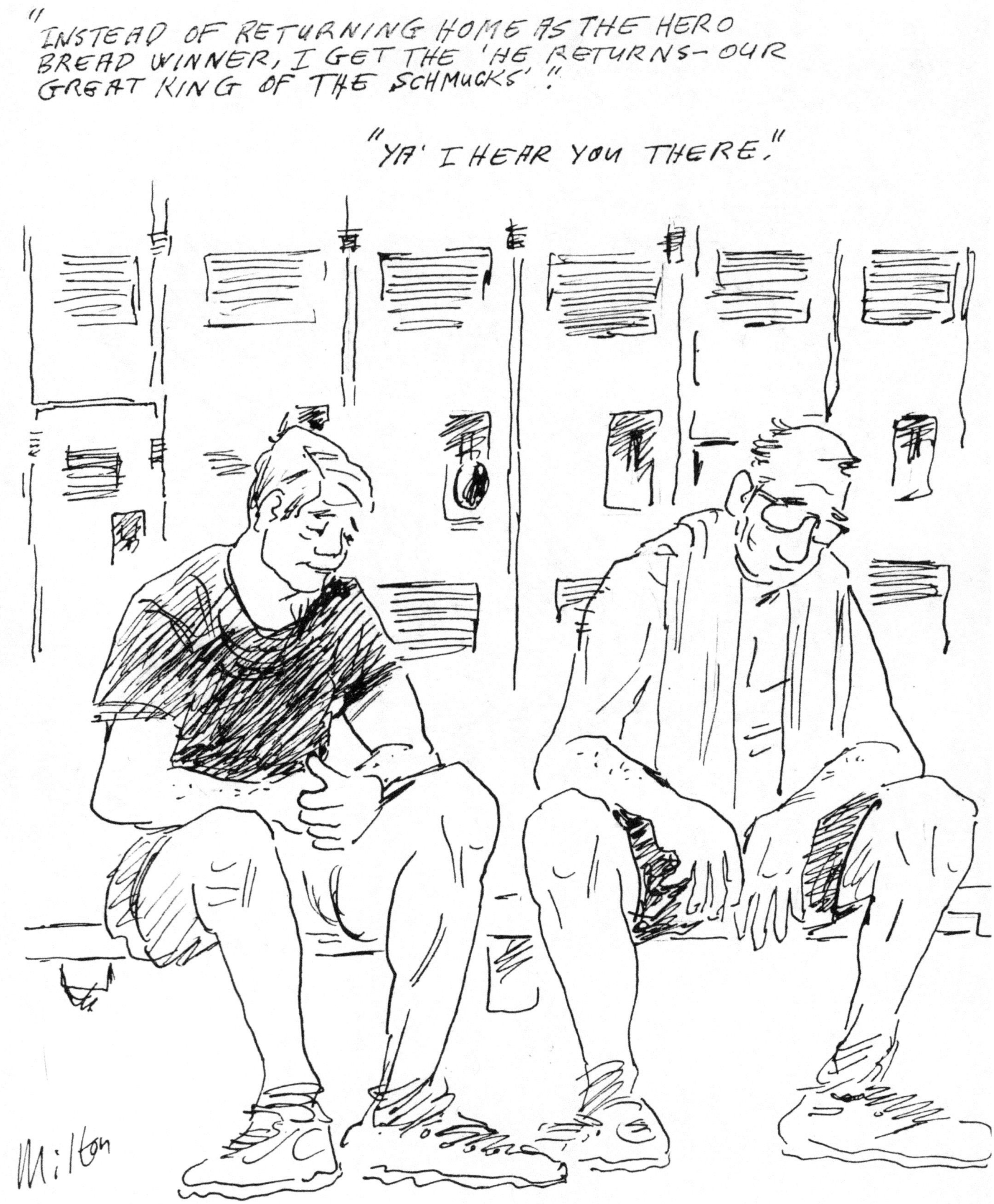
"INSTEAD OF RETURNING HOME AS THE HERO BREAD WINNER, I GET THE 'HE RETURNS- OUR GREAT KING OF THE SCHMUCKS'!"
"YA' I HEAR YOU THERE."
Milton

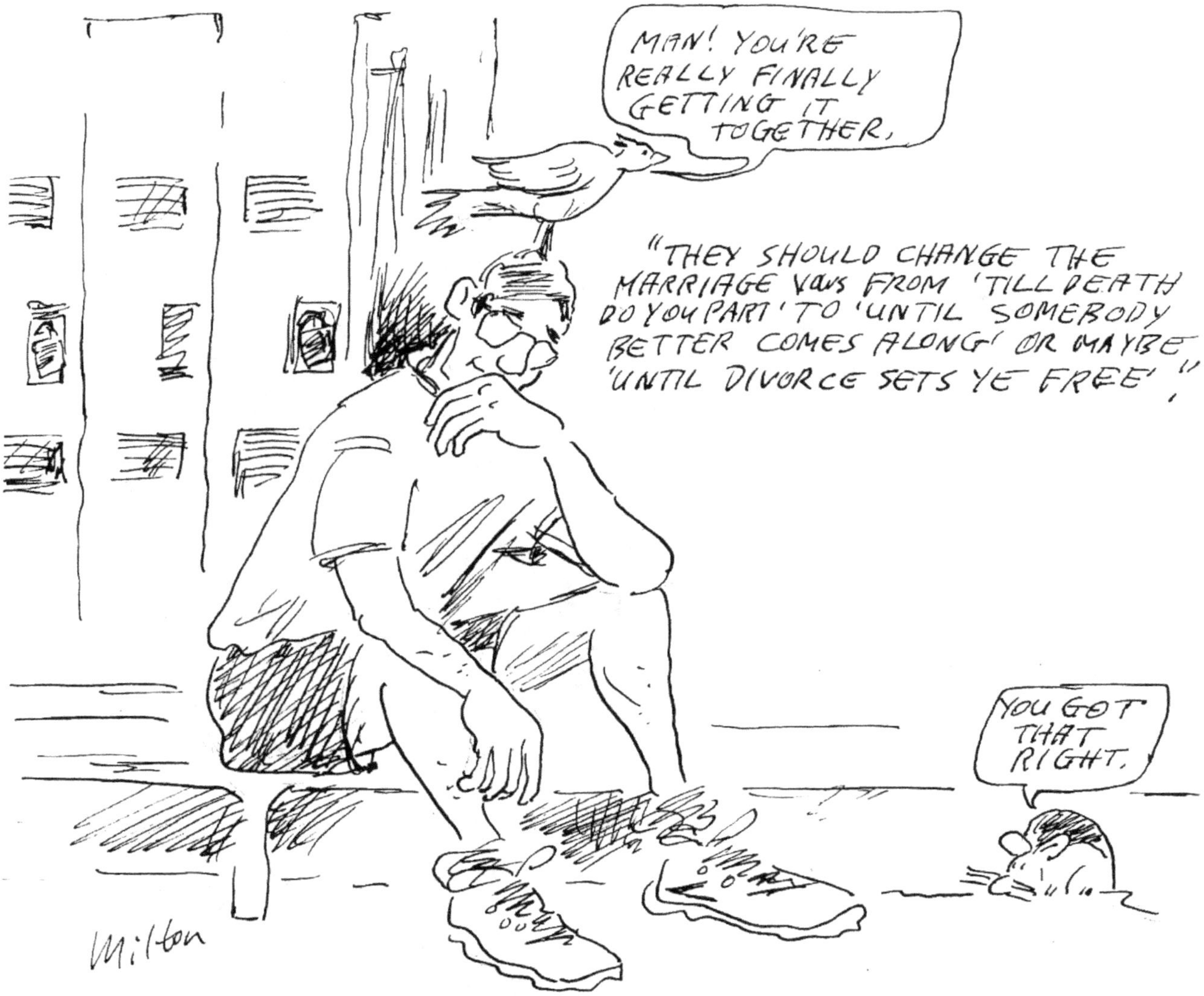
MAN! YOU'RE REALLY FINALLY GETTING IT TOGETHER.
"THEY SHOULD CHANGE THE MARRIAGE VOWS FROM 'TILL DEATH DO YOU PART' TO 'UNTIL SOMEBODY BETTER COMES ALONG' OR MAYBE 'UNTIL DIVORCE SETS YE FREE'."
YOU GOT THAT RIGHT.
Milton

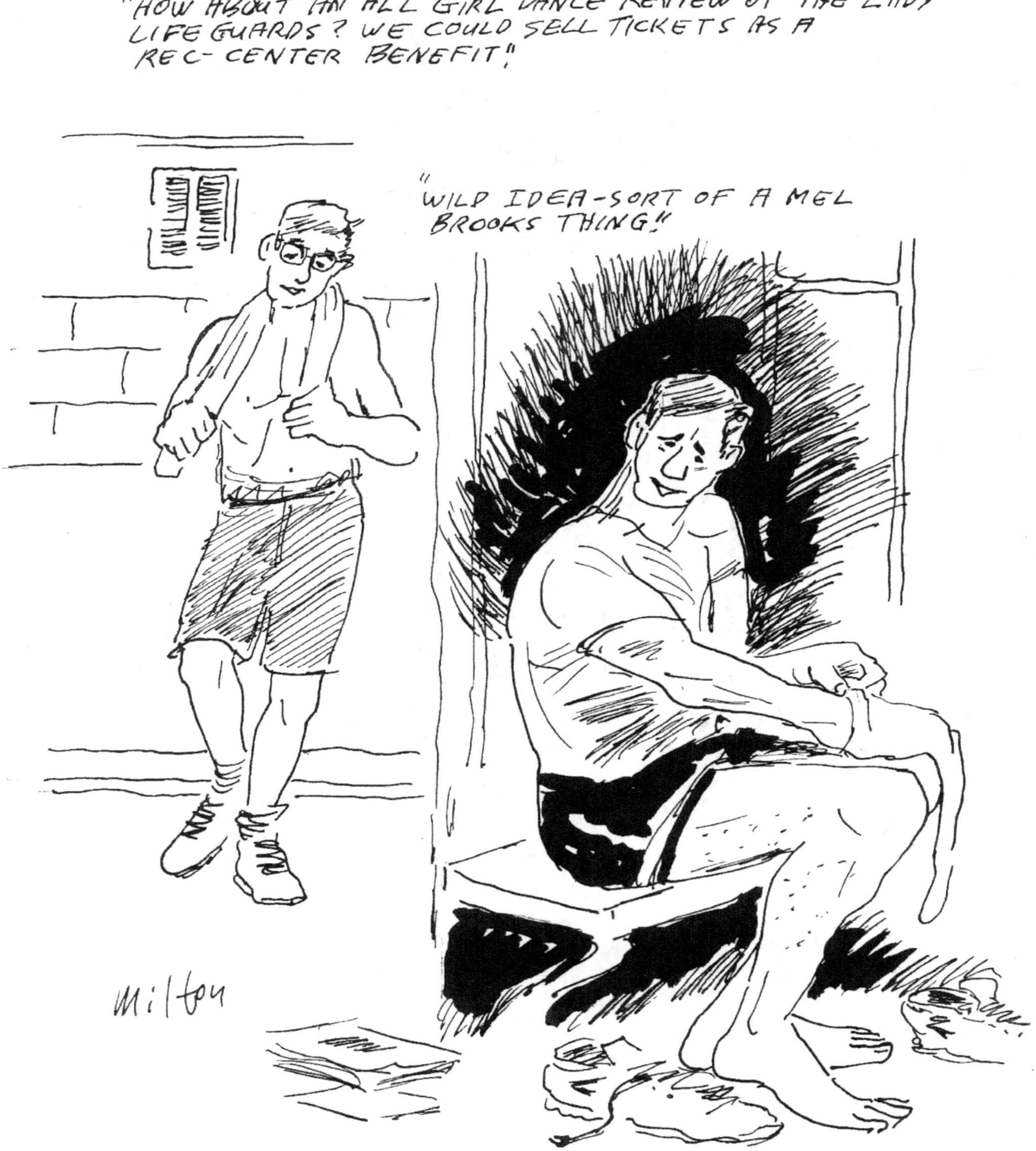
"HOW ABOUT AN ALL GIRL DANCE REVIEW OF THE LADY LIFE GUARDS? WE COULD SELL TICKETS AS A REC-CENTER BENEFIT."
"WILD IDEA-SORT OF A MEL BROOKS THING!"
milton

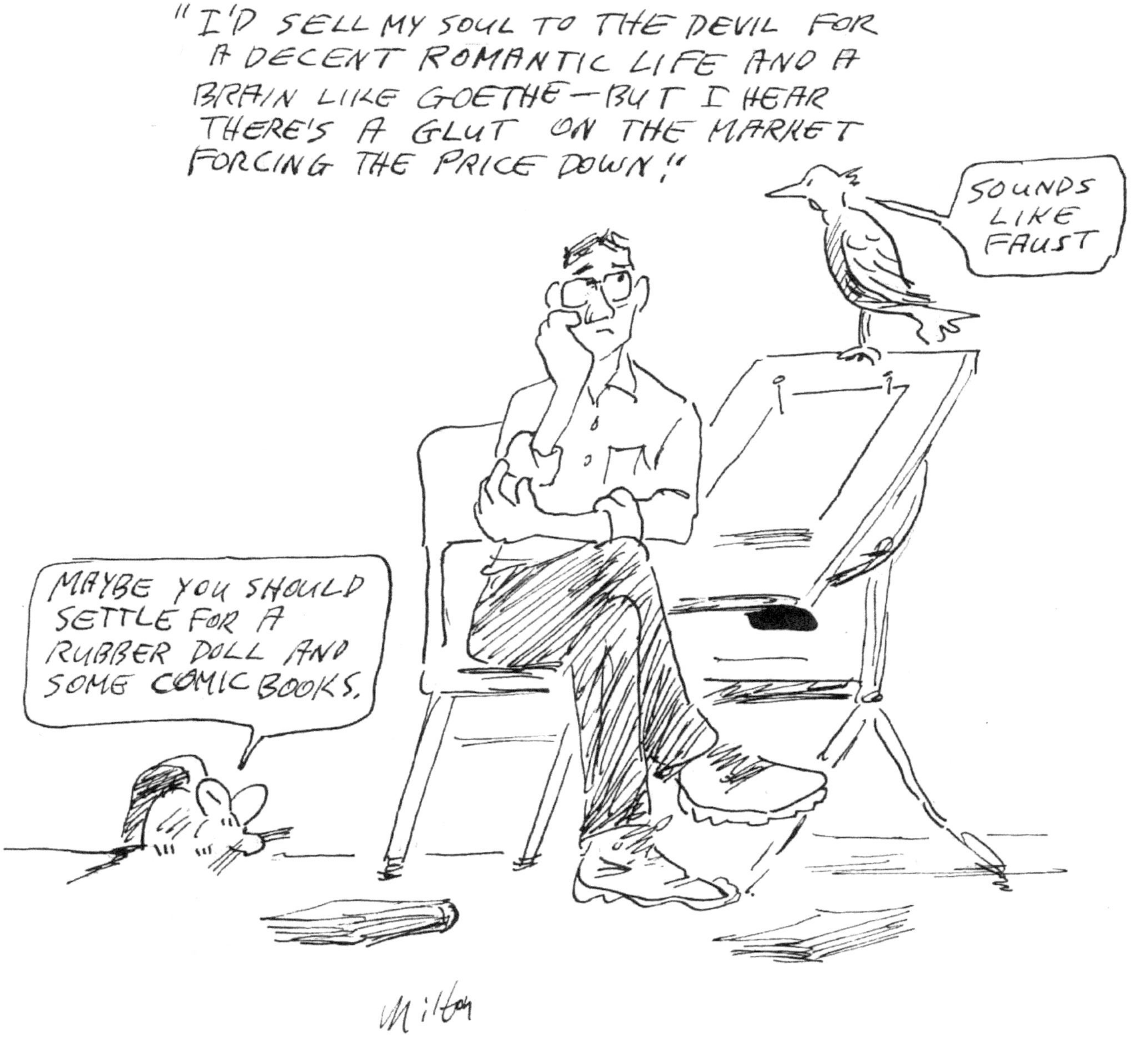
"I'D SELL MY SOUL TO THE DEVIL FOR A DECENT ROMANTIC LIFE AND A BRAIN LIKE GOETHE—BUT I HEAR THERE'S A GLUT ON THE MARKET FORCING THE PRICE DOWN!"
SOUNDS LIKE FAUST
MAYBE YOU SHOULD SETTLE FOR A RUBBER DOLL AND SOME COMIC BOOKS.
Milton

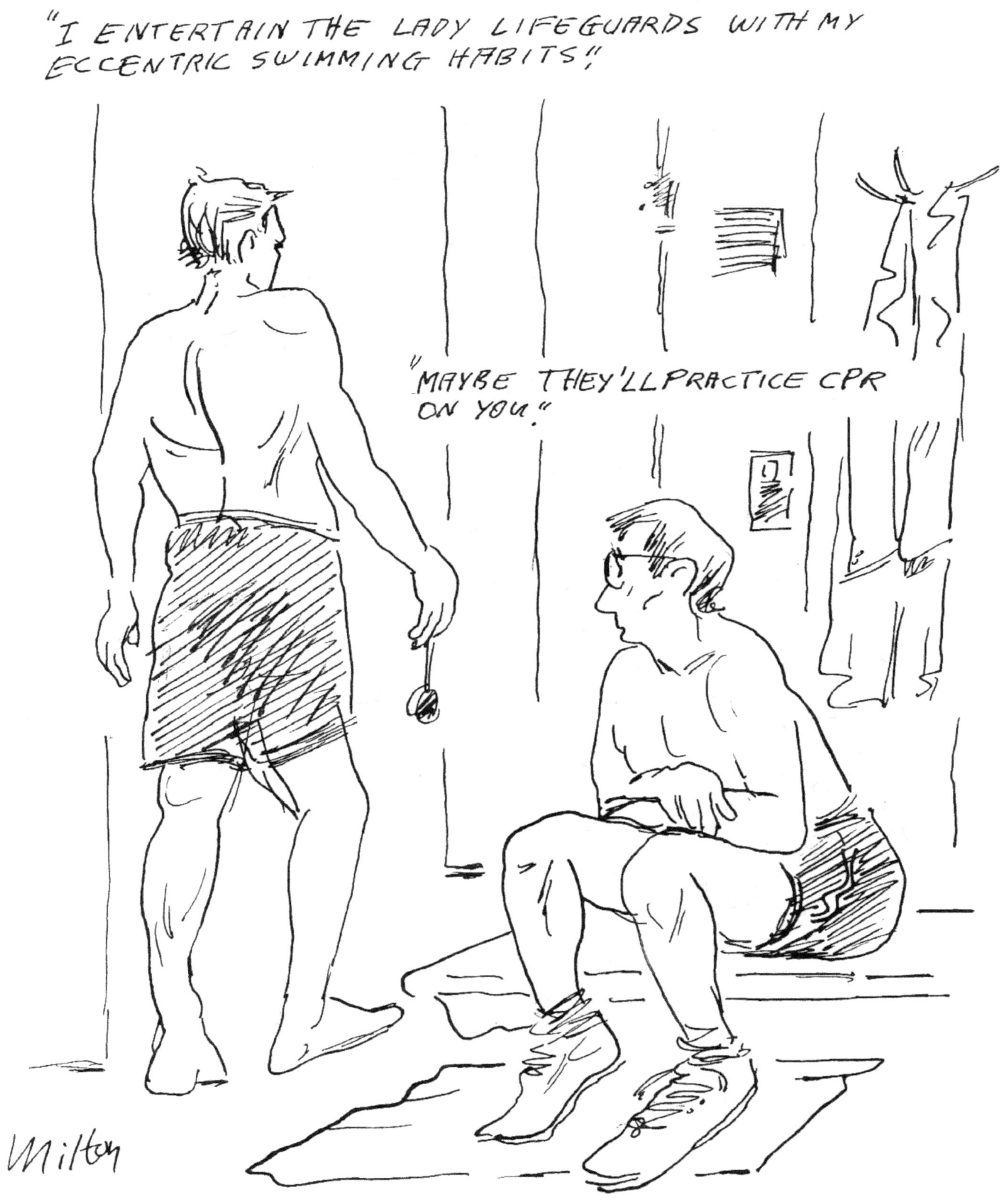
"I ENTERTAIN THE LADY LIFEGUARDS WITH MY ECCENTRIC SWIMMING HABITS!"
"MAYBE THEY'LL PRACTICE CPR ON YOU."
Milton

A NEW LIFEGUARD SHOWS UP AT THE POOL AND THE LAP LANES TRIPLE IN BUSINESS WITH LOVESICK JOCKS...

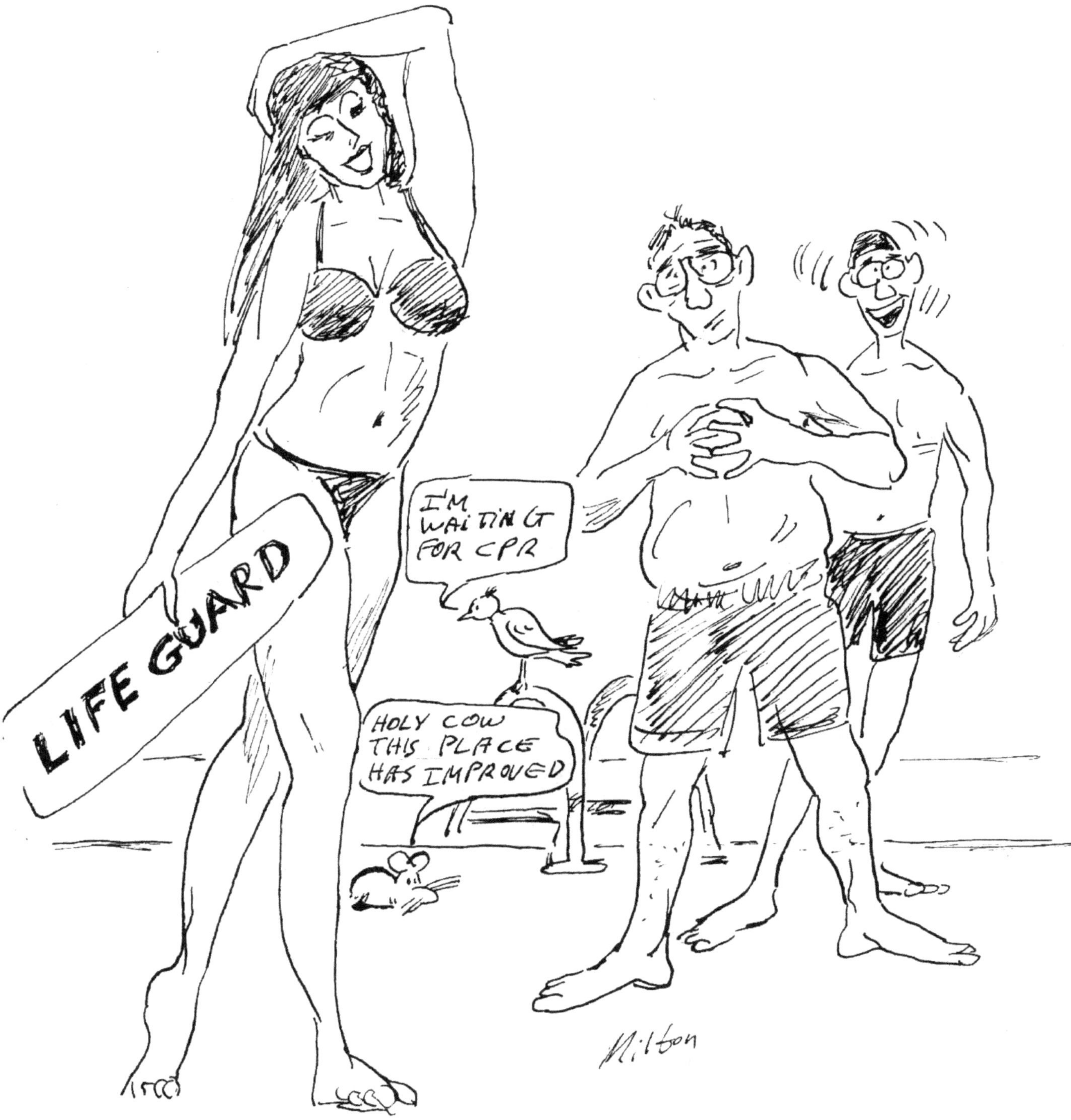
LIFE GUARD
I'M WAITING FOR CPR
HOLY COW THIS PLACE HAS IMPROVED
Milton

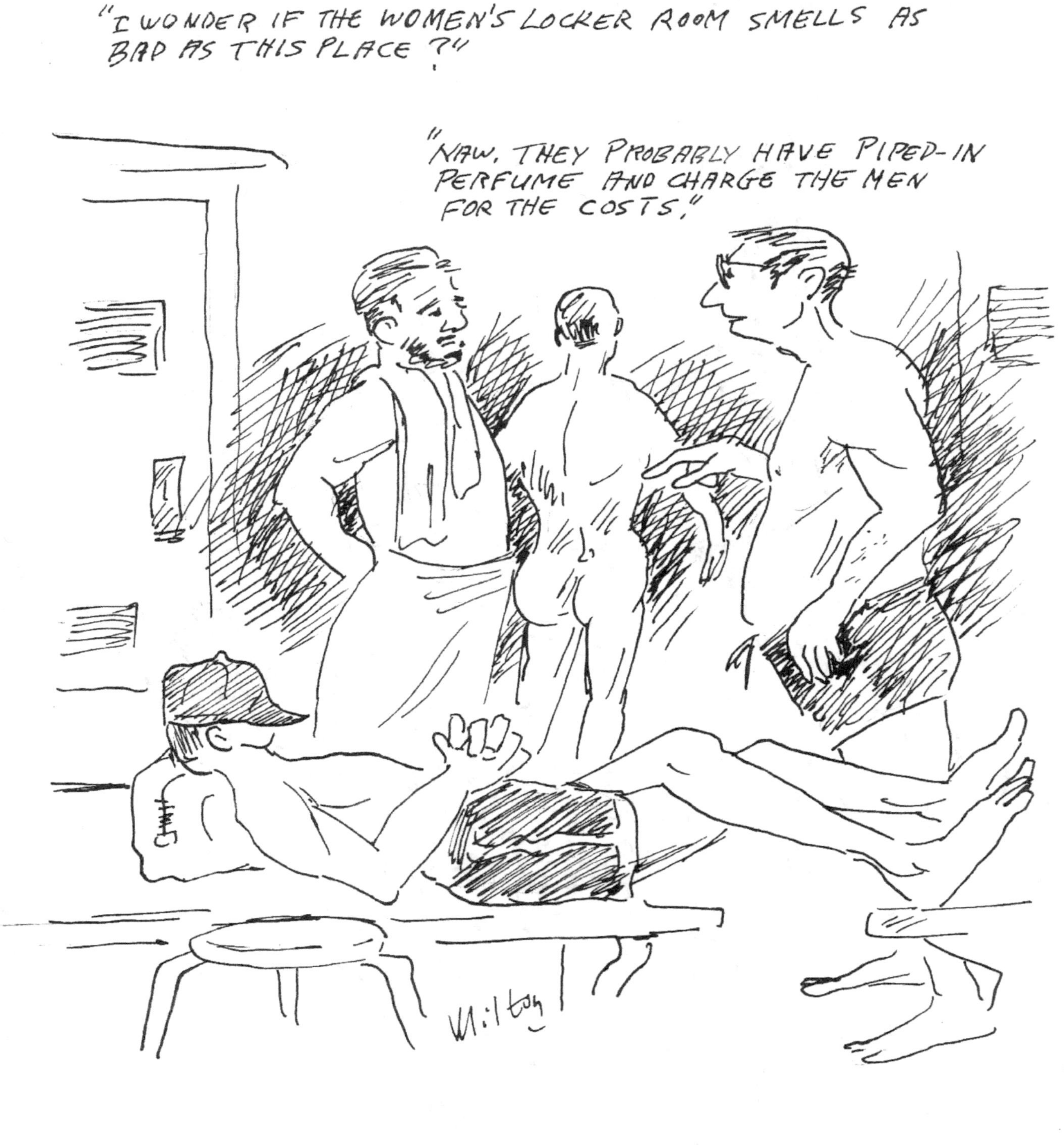
"I WONDER IF THE WOMEN'S LOCKER ROOM SMELLS AS BAD AS THIS PLACE?"
"NAW, THEY PROBABLY HAVE PIPED-IN PERFUME AND CHARGE THE MEN FOR THE COSTS."
Milton

"THE MEN'S LOCKER ROOM - THE HEART STENT - TRANSPLANT AND BY-PASS CAPITOL OF THE WORLD."

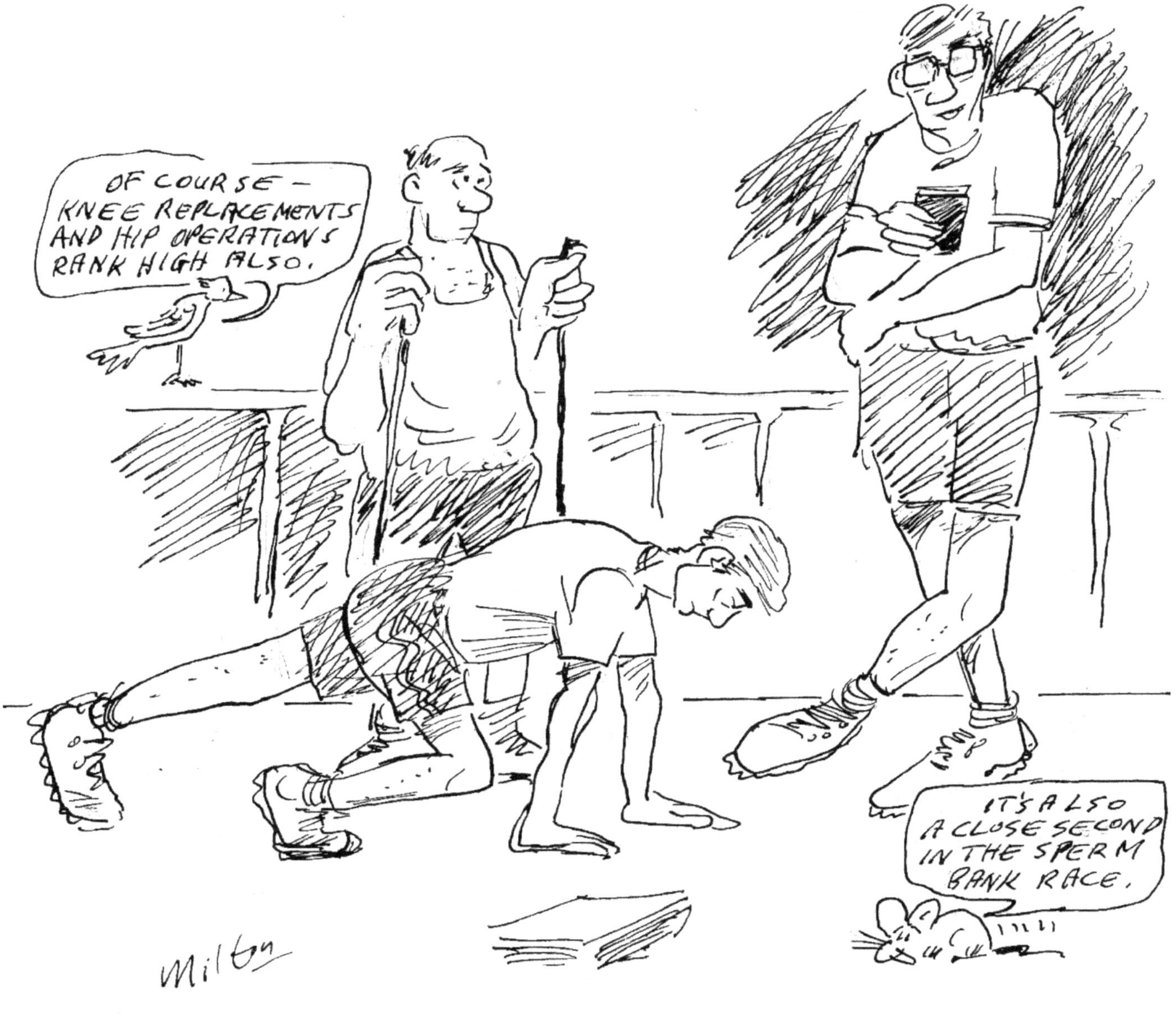
OF COURSE - KNEE REPLACEMENTS AND HIP OPERATIONS RANK HIGH ALSO.
IT'S ALSO A CLOSE SECOND IN THE SPERM BANK RACE.
Milton

"WE'VE BEEN MARRIED TWENTY TWO YEARS—NOW SHE WANT'S OUT. I CAN'T SEEM TO DO ANYTHING THAT PLEASES HER. THE CHILDREN TURN AWAY FROM ME."

"GEEZ, I'M GLAD I'M SINGLE."

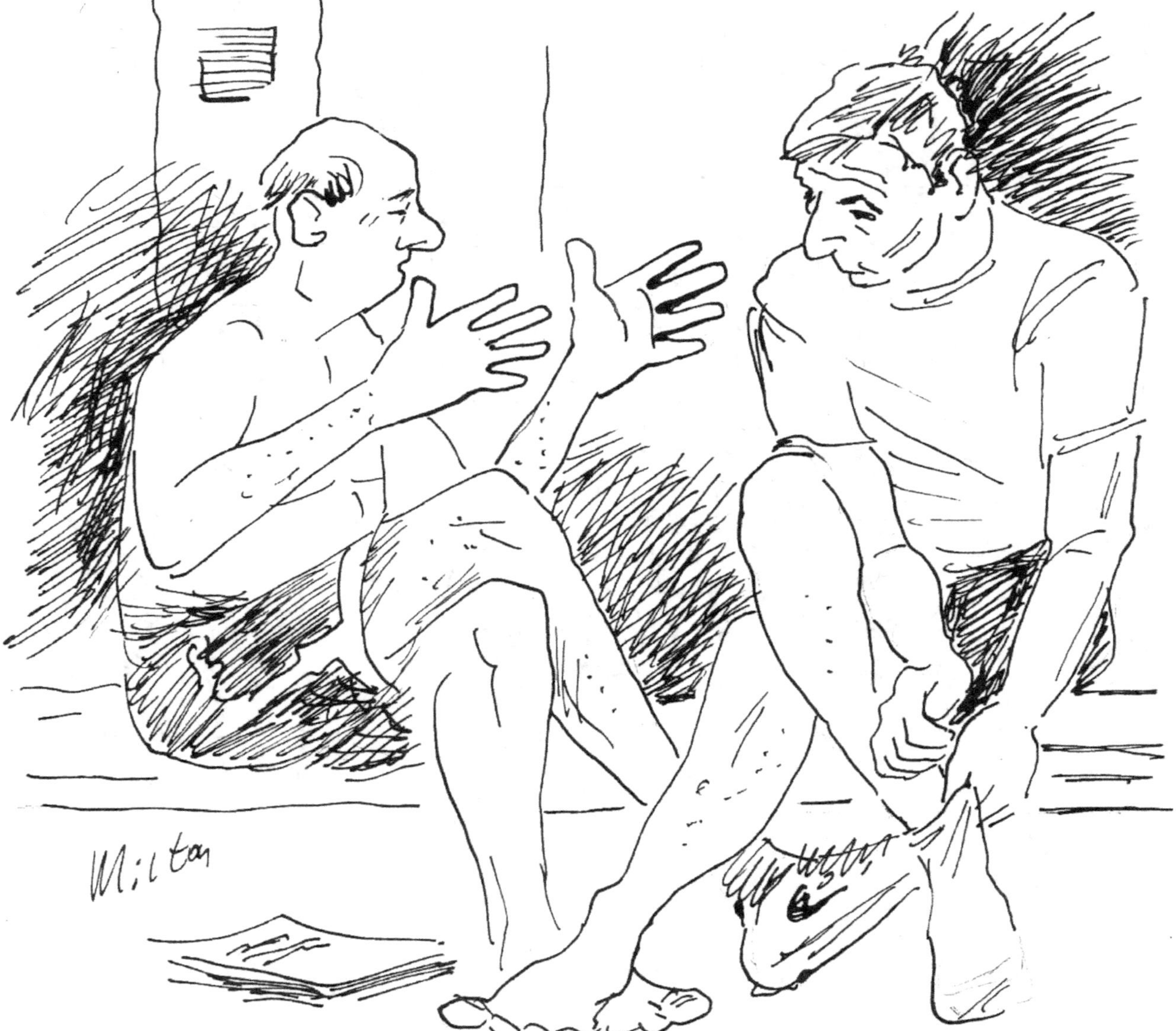
Milton

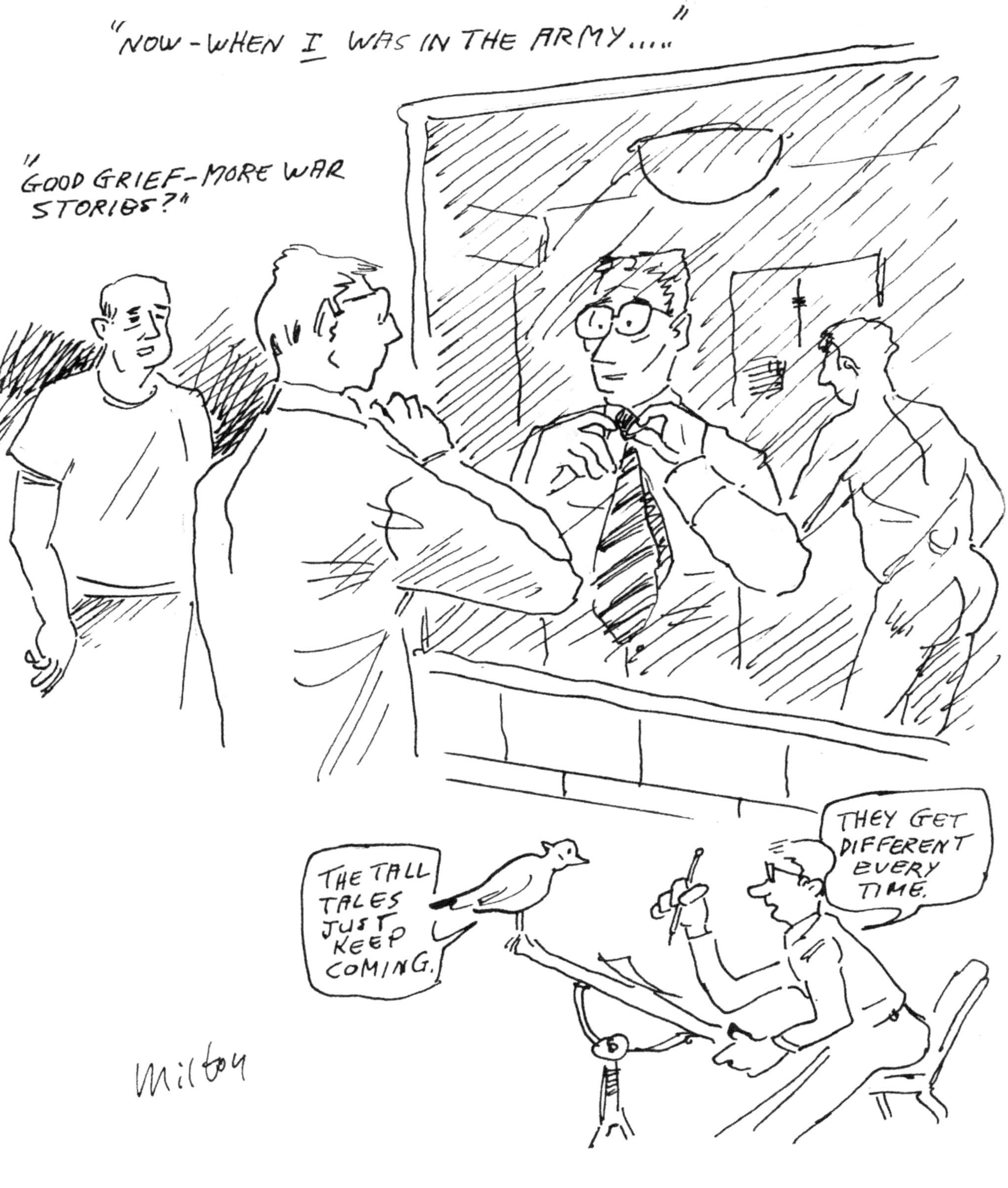
"NOW - WHEN I WAS IN THE ARMY....."
"GOOD GRIEF - MORE WAR STORIES?"
THE TALL TALES JUST KEEP COMING.
THEY GET DIFFERENT EVERY TIME.
Milton

"AS SOON AS I'M PASSED UP ON THE TRAIL BY SOME OLD GAL WITH A WALKER- I'M QUITTING RUNNING."

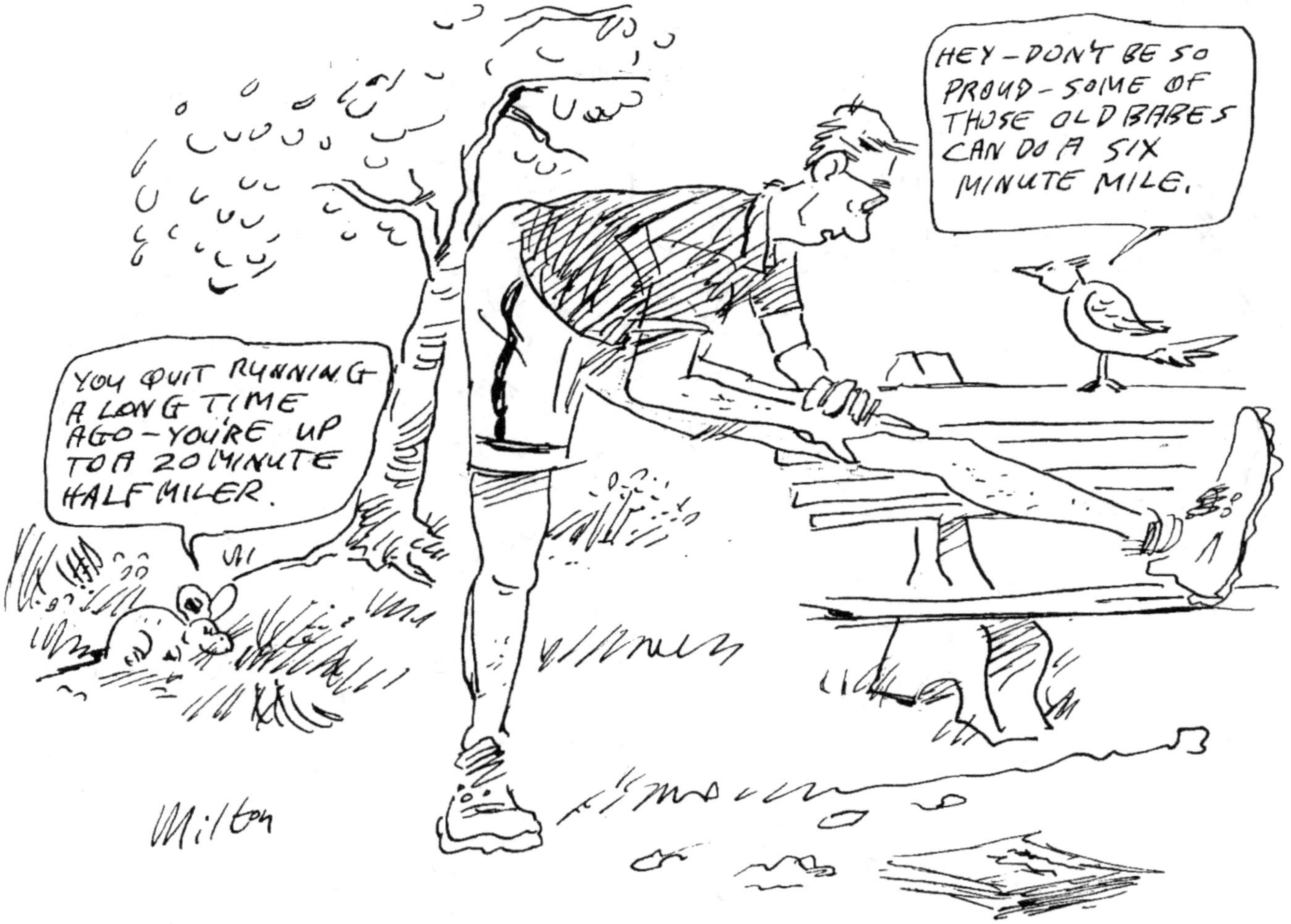
HEY-DON'T BE SO PROUD-SOME OF THOSE OLD BABES CAN DO A SIX MINUTE MILE.
YOU QUIT RUNNING A LONG TIME AGO-YOU'RE UP TO A 20 MINUTE HALF MILER.
Milton

MOST HACYNEYED AND TRITE PHRASES HEARD IN THE MEN'S LOCKER ROOM

1. KEEP ACTIVE
2. YOU'RE NOT OLD .... WHEN DID YOU RETIRE?
3. EVERYONE MUST DIE
4. HOW'S IT GOIN?
5. HANG IN THERE – DO WHAT YOU CAN
6. YOU'RE STILL IN GOOD SHAPE
7. MY COUSIN (ETC.) IS NINTY AND HE.....
8. HOW OLD ARE YOU?
9. WHERE ARE YOU FROM?
10. WHAT DID YOU DO BEFORE YOU RETIRED?
11. DID THE CARDINALS WIN LAST NIGHT?
12. HOW DID MIZOU DO AGAINST KANSAS.. ETC.?
13. WHAT'S YOUR PSA COUNT?
14. HAVE A NICE DAY – OR HAVE A GOOD ONE *

POSSIBLE SUBSTITUTES FOR HACKNEYED TRITE SAYINGS

1. CHEERIO – CHEERS – AUF WIEDERSEHEN – CHOW
2. WATCH OUT FOR THE REPUBLICANS OUT THERE – IT'S A JUNGLE
3. DRIVE WITH A VENGENCE
4. DON'T HURRY BACK – YOU'ALL HEE-A?
5. GOD'SPEED
6. TALLY – HO
7. KISS MY A.....
8. FARE – THEE – WELL
9. SAFE JOURNEY
10. SEE YOU AT HOOTERS
11. DON'T PUT YOUR TURN SIGNAL ON AT McDONALD'S
12. BE ALERT FOR THE JIHADISTS AND TALIBAN OUT THERE
13. FART PROUDLY *

THE LIST COULD GO ON AND ON.
YA – THE CRAP JUST KEEPS COMING
milton

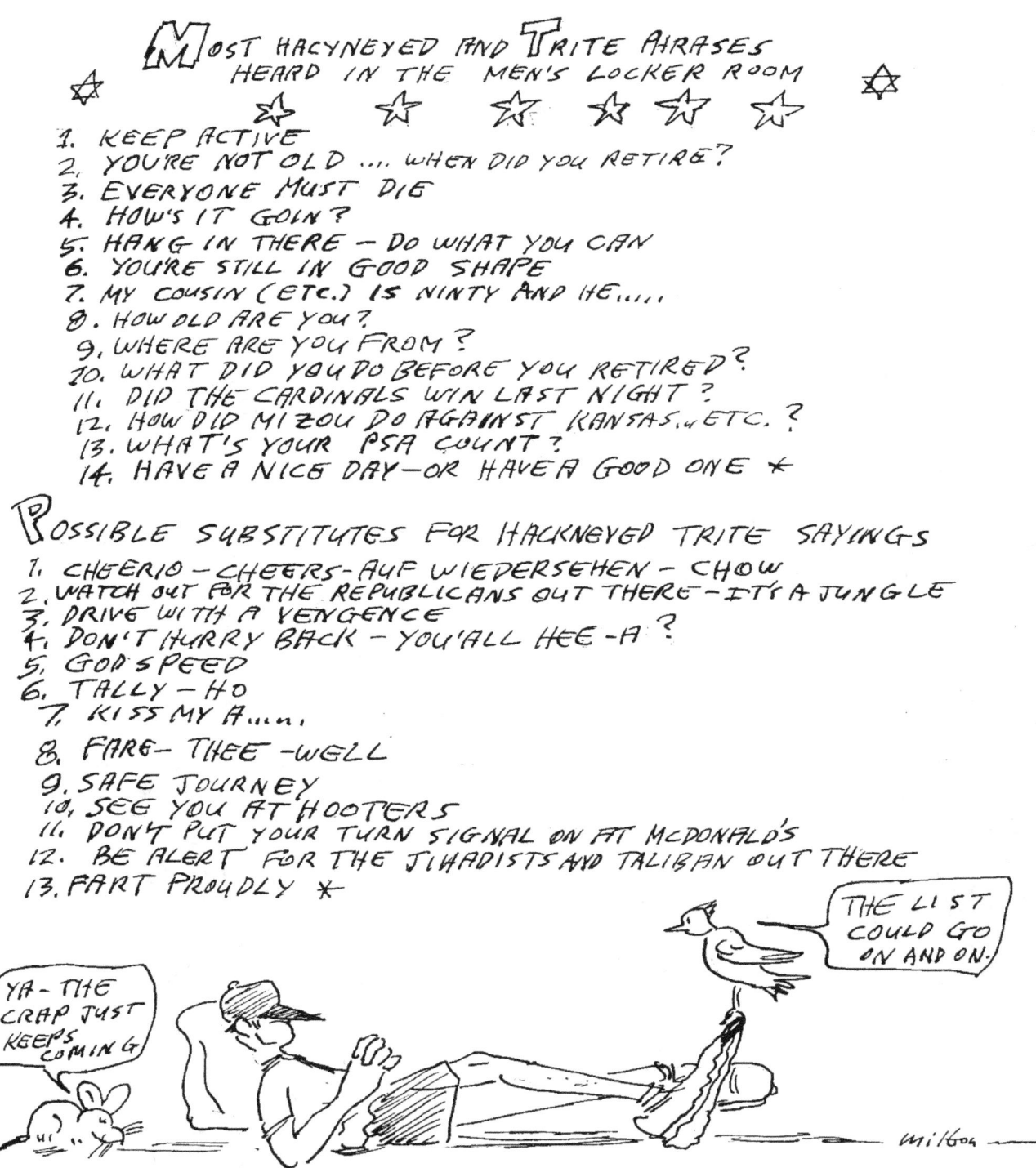

* TOP RANKED – NUMBER ONE.

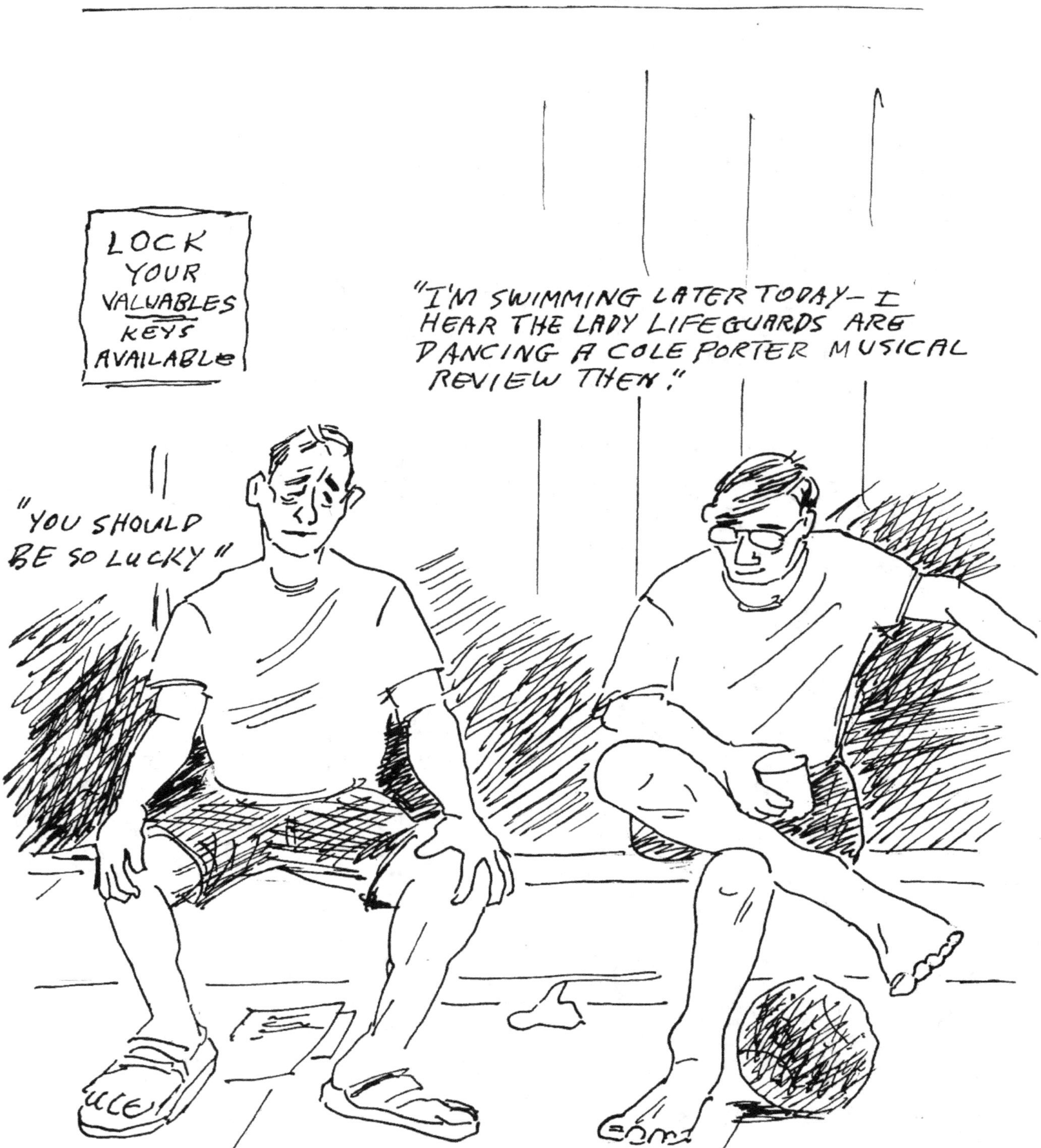
LOCK YOUR VALUABLES
KEYS AVAILABLE
"I'M SWIMMING LATER TODAY- I HEAR THE LADY LIFEGUARDS ARE DANCING A COLE PORTER MUSICAL REVIEW THEN."
"YOU SHOULD BE SO LUCKY"
Milton

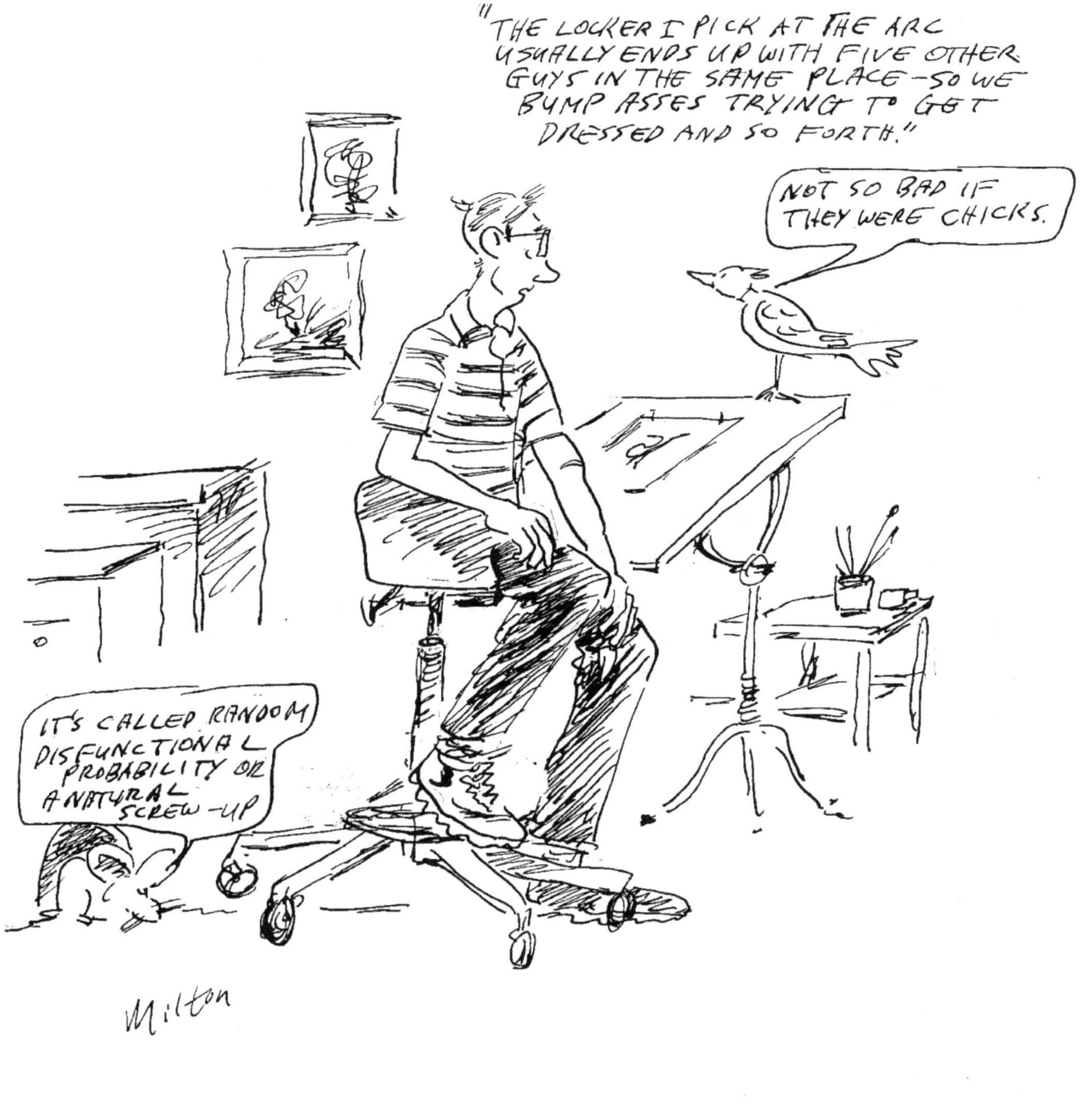
"THE LOCKER I PICK AT THE ARC USUALLY ENDS UP WITH FIVE OTHER GUYS IN THE SAME PLACE—SO WE BUMP ASSES TRYING TO GET DRESSED AND SO FORTH."
NOT SO BAD IF THEY WERE CHICKS.
IT'S CALLED RANDOM DISFUNCTIONAL PROBABILITY OR A NATURAL SCREW-UP
Milton

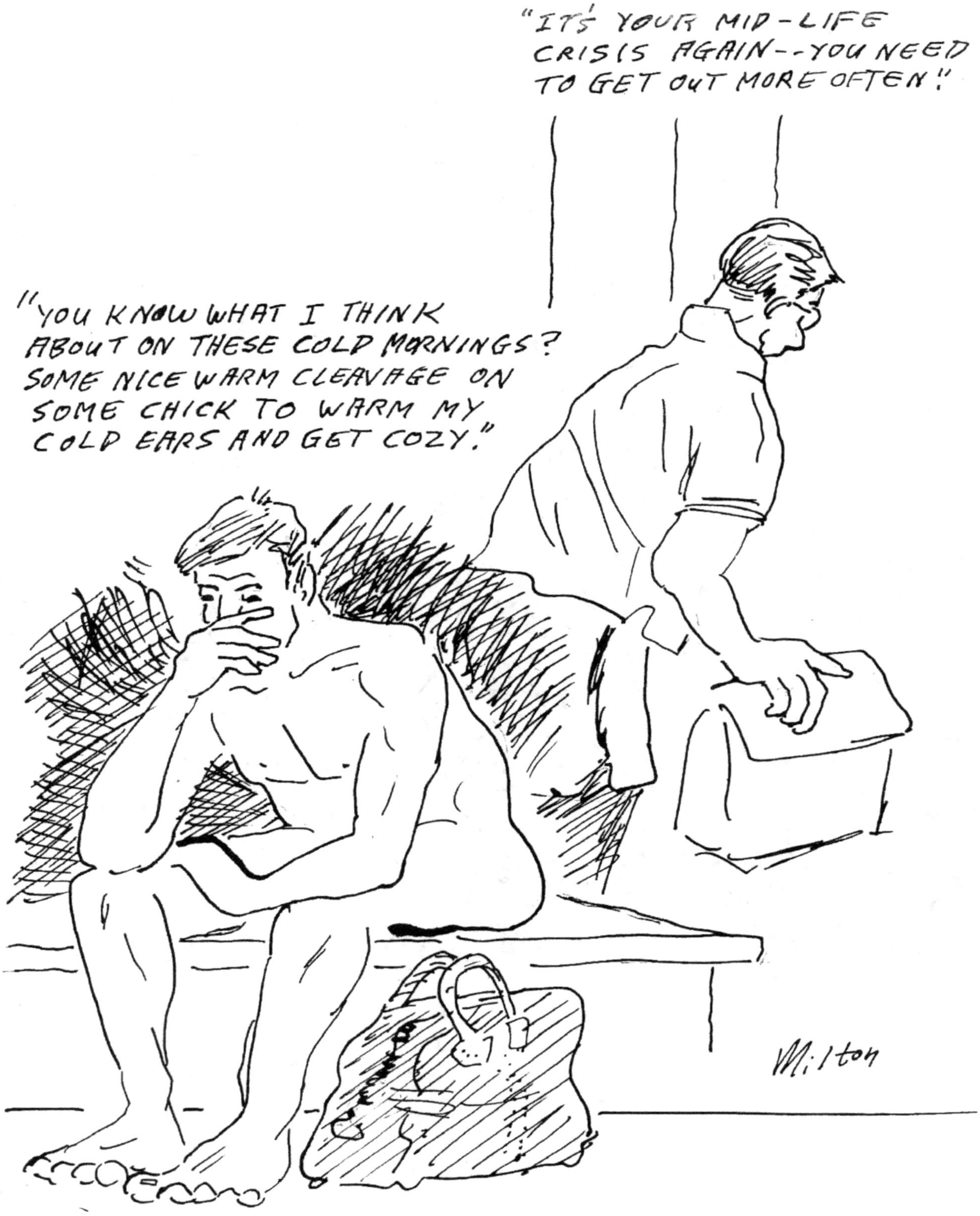
"IT'S YOUR MID-LIFE CRISIS AGAIN--YOU NEED TO GET OUT MORE OFTEN!"
"YOU KNOW WHAT I THINK ABOUT ON THESE COLD MORNINGS? SOME NICE WARM CLEAVAGE ON SOME CHICK TO WARM MY COLD EARS AND GET COZY."
Milton

"SOME OF THE GUYS THINK I SHOULD TRY OUT FOR THE SENIOR OLYMPICS!"

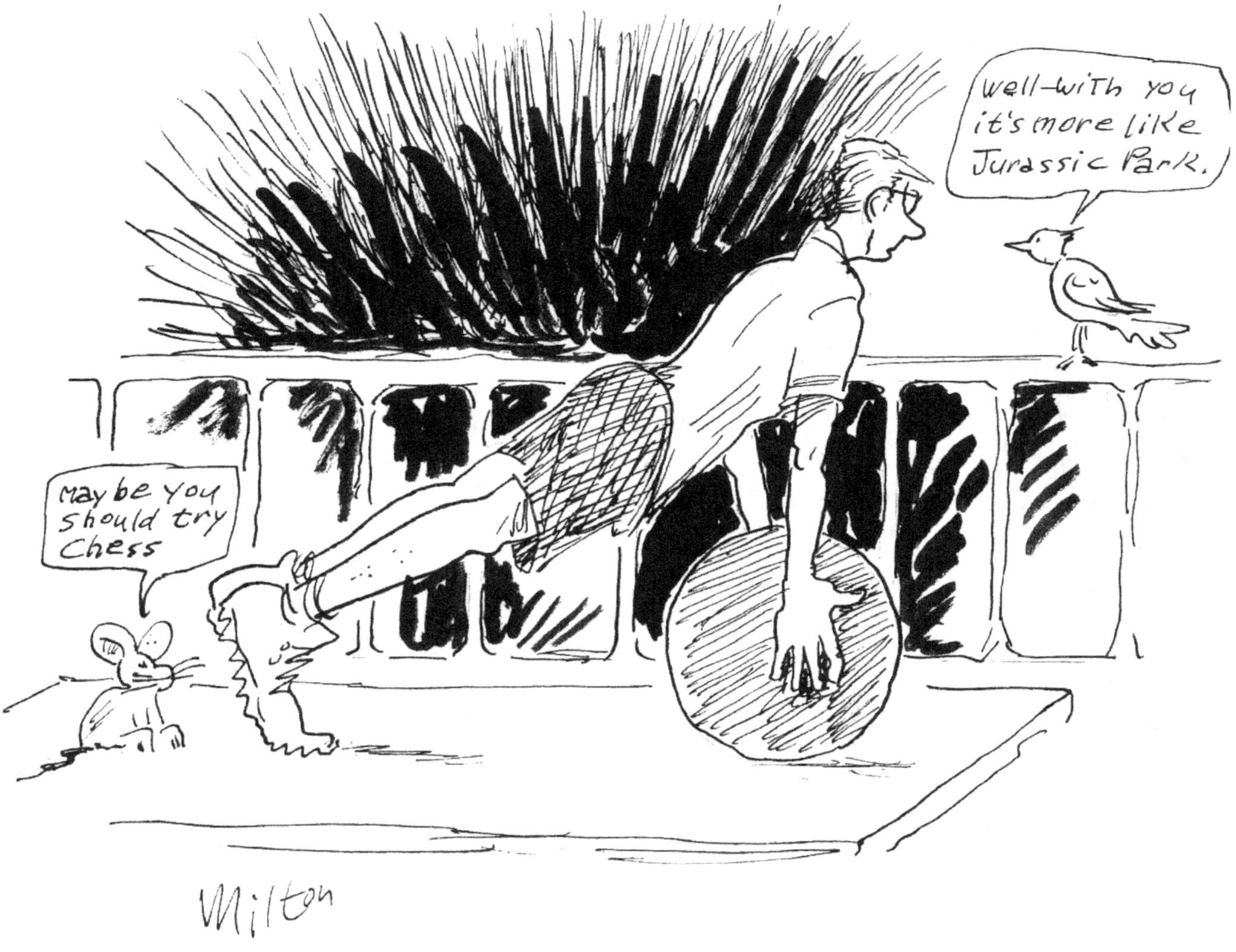
maybe you should try chess
well-with you it's more like Jurassic Park.
Milton

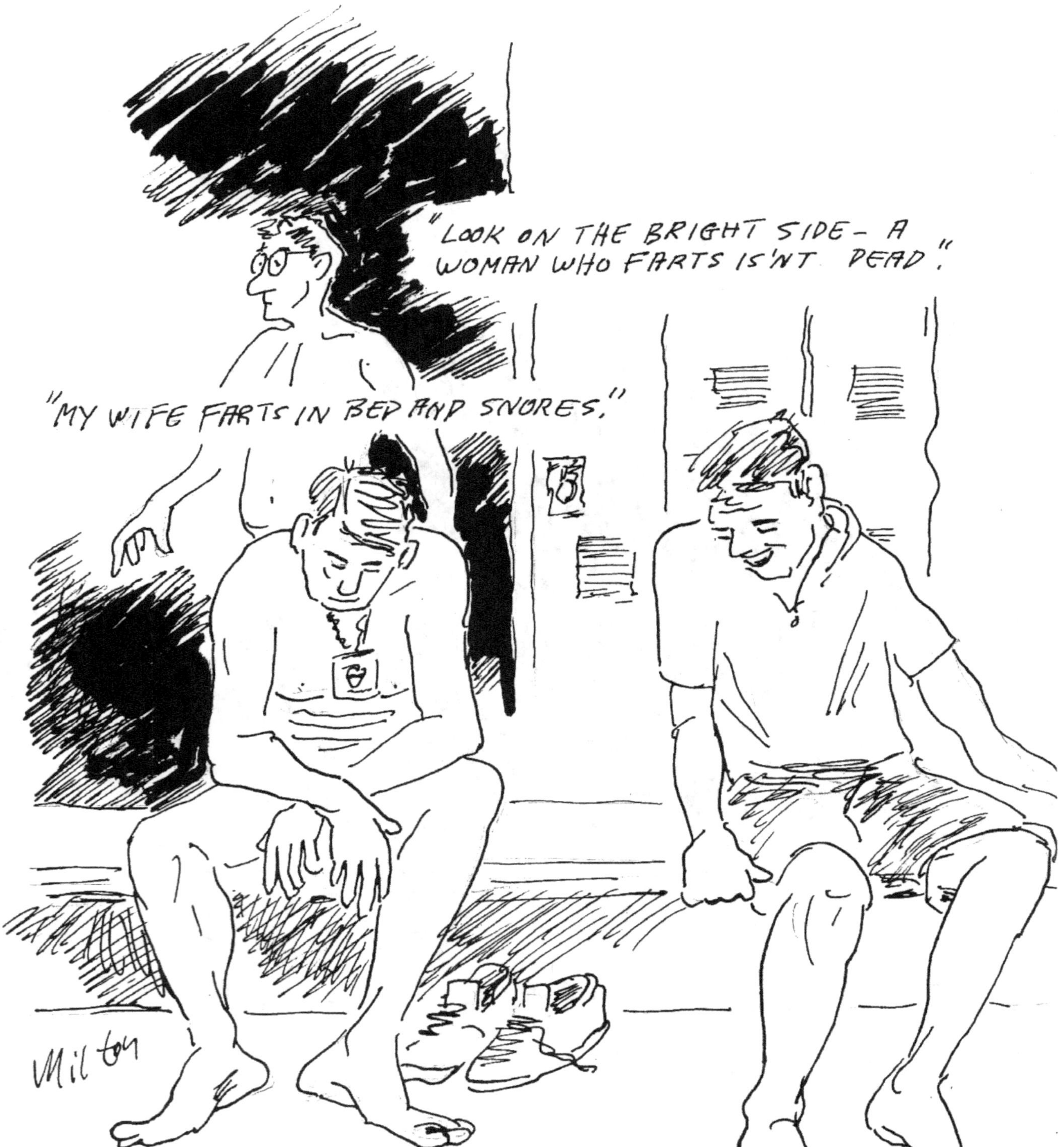
"LOOK ON THE BRIGHT SIDE - A WOMAN WHO FARTS IS'NT DEAD."
"MY WIFE FARTS IN BED AND SNORES."
Milton

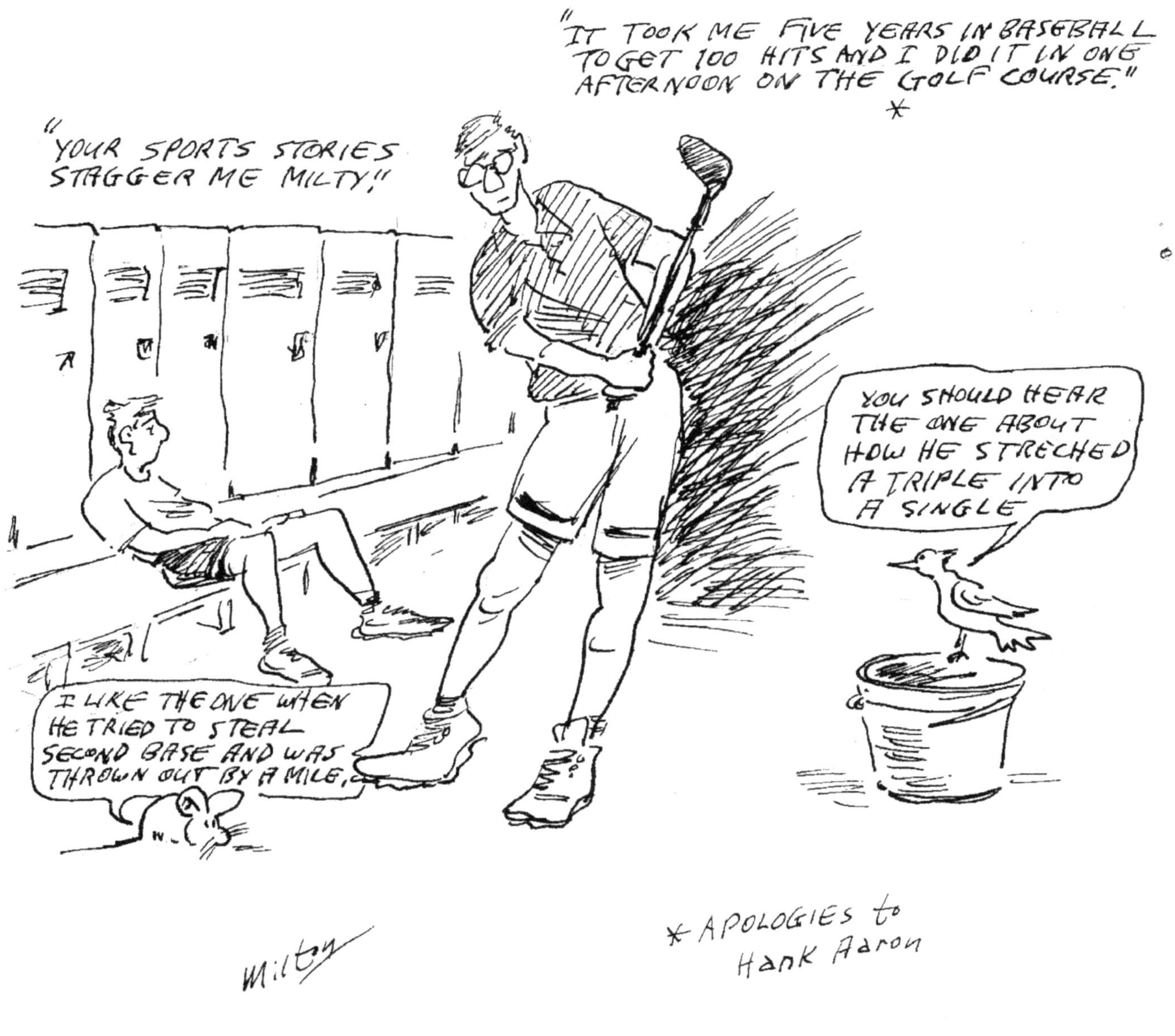
"YOUR SPORTS STORIES STAGGER ME MILTY!"
"IT TOOK ME FIVE YEARS IN BASEBALL TO GET 100 HITS AND I DID IT IN ONE AFTERNOON ON THE GOLF COURSE." *
YOU SHOULD HEAR THE ONE ABOUT HOW HE STRECHED A TRIPLE INTO A SINGLE
I LIKE THE ONE WHEN HE TRIED TO STEAL SECOND BASE AND WAS THROWN OUT BY A MILE.
Milty
* APOLOGIES to Hank Aaron

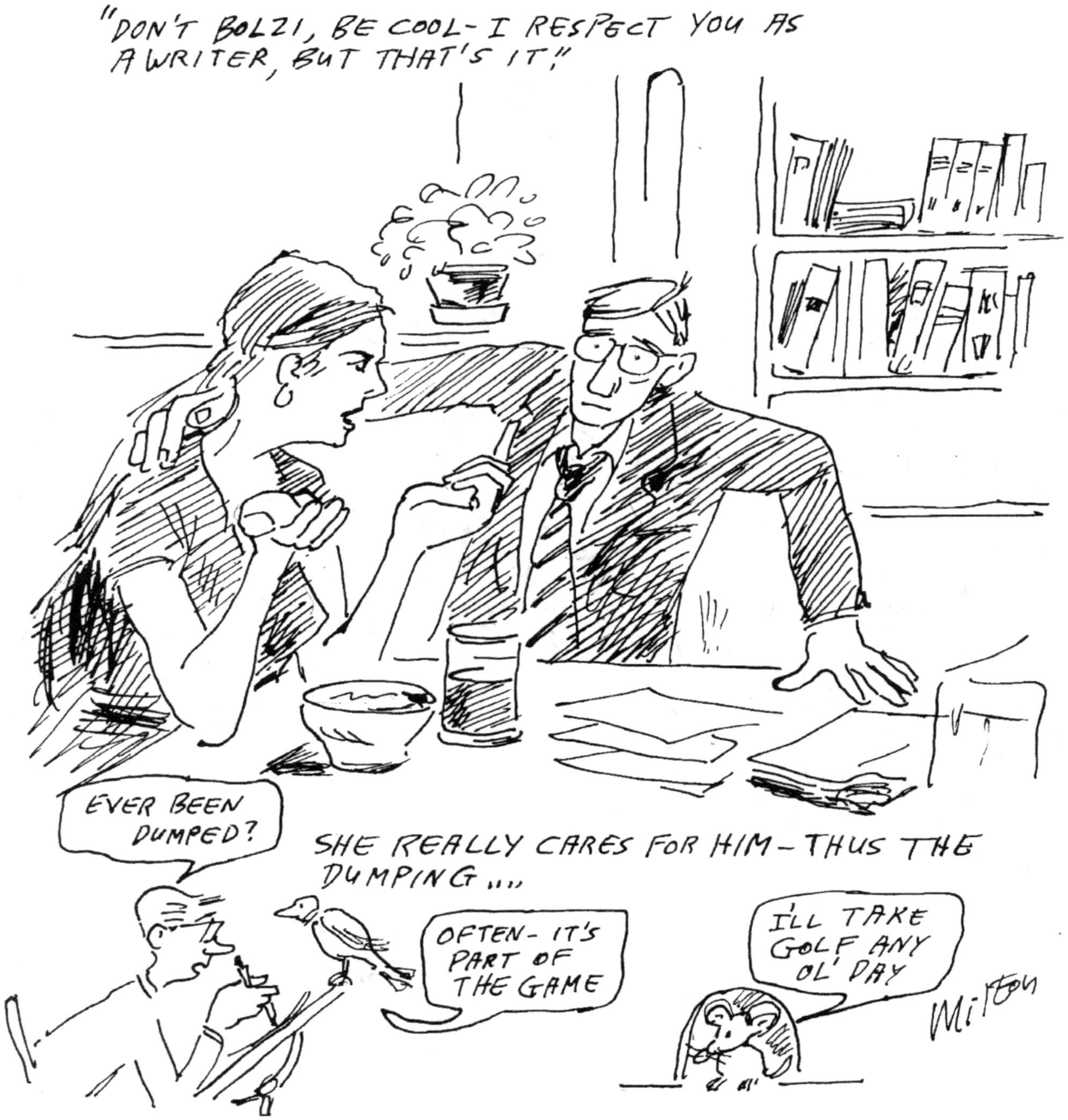
"DON'T BOLZI, BE COOL- I RESPECT YOU AS A WRITER, BUT THAT'S IT!"
EVER BEEN DUMPED?
SHE REALLY CARES FOR HIM-THUS THE DUMPING....
OFTEN- IT'S PART OF THE GAME
I'LL TAKE GOLF ANY OL' DAY
Milton

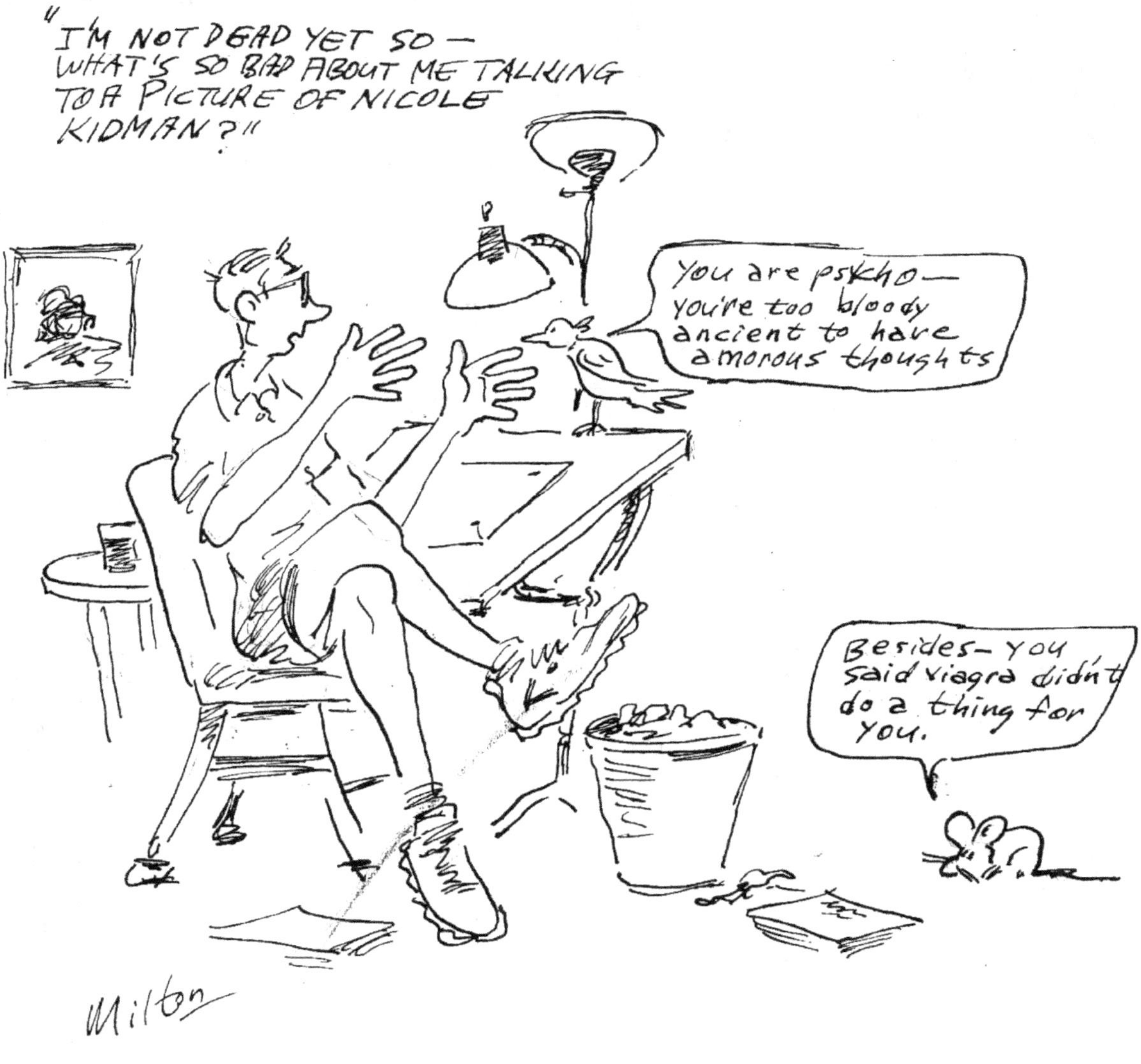
"I'M NOT DEAD YET SO — WHAT'S SO BAD ABOUT ME TALKING TO A PICTURE OF NICOLE KIDMAN?"
You are pskho— you're too bloody ancient to have amorous thoughts
Besides— you said viagra didn't do a thing for you.
Milton

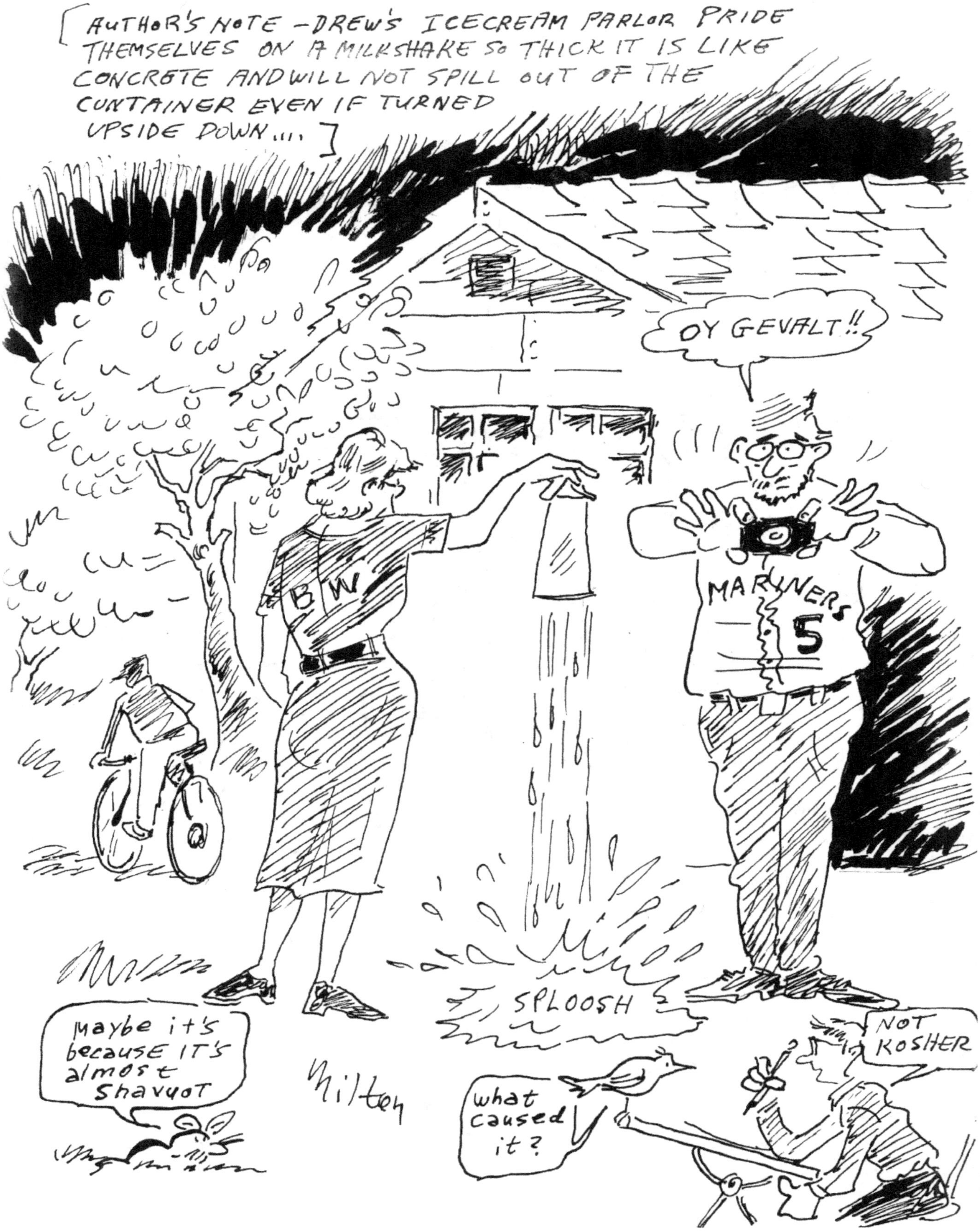
[AUTHOR'S NOTE – DREW'S ICECREAM PARLOR PRIDE THEMSELVES ON A MILKSHAKE SO THICK IT IS LIKE CONCRETE AND WILL NOT SPILL OUT OF THE CONTAINER EVEN IF TURNED UPSIDE DOWN....]
OY GEVALT!!
BW
MARINERS
5
SPLOOSH
maybe it's because IT'S almost Shavuot
Milton
NOT KOSHER
what caused it?

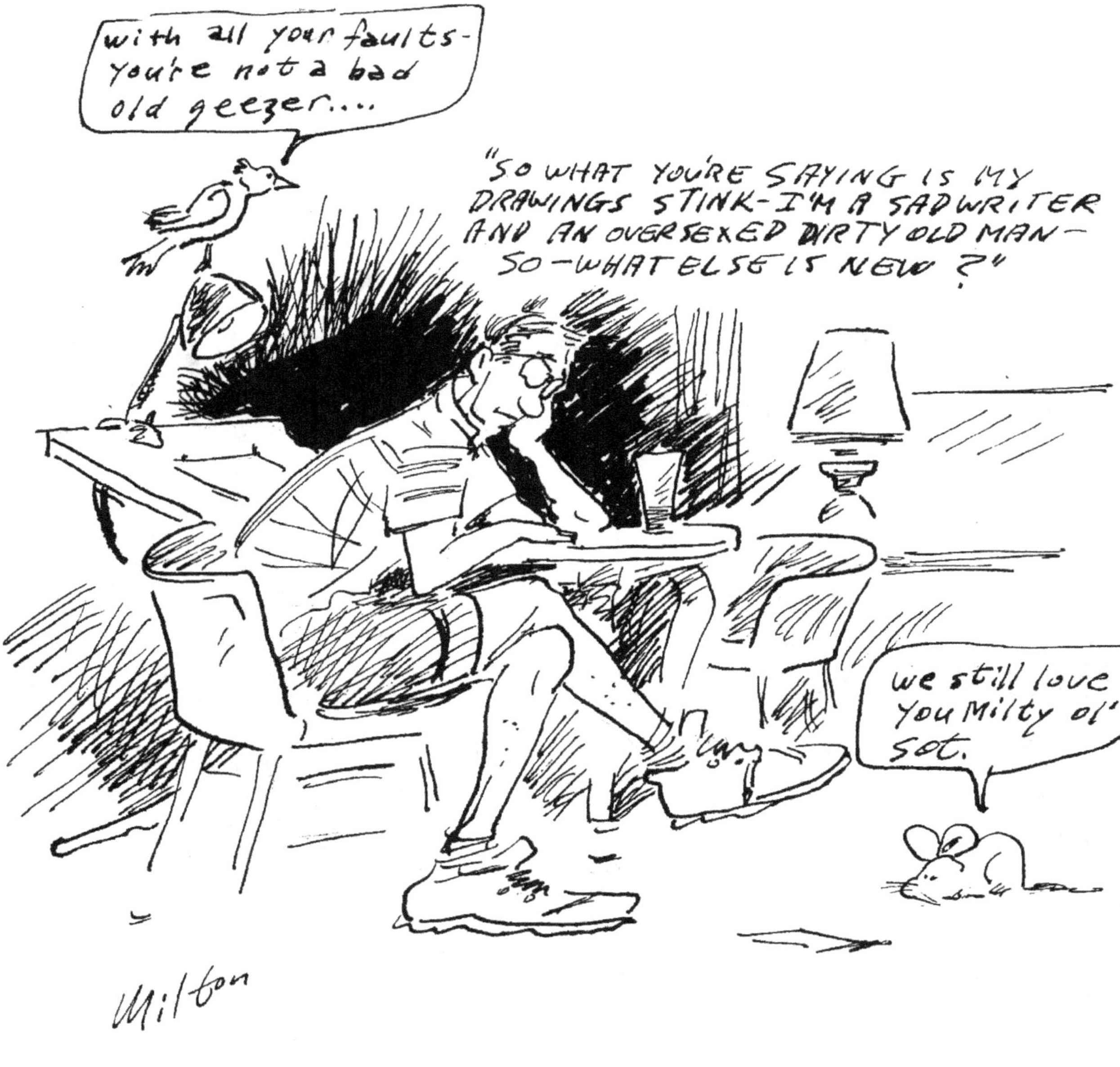
with all your faults- you're not a bad old geezer....
"SO WHAT YOU'RE SAYING IS MY DRAWINGS STINK-I'M A SADWRITER AND AN OVERSEXED DIRTY OLD MAN- SO-WHAT ELSE IS NEW ?"
we still love you Milty ol' sot.
Milton

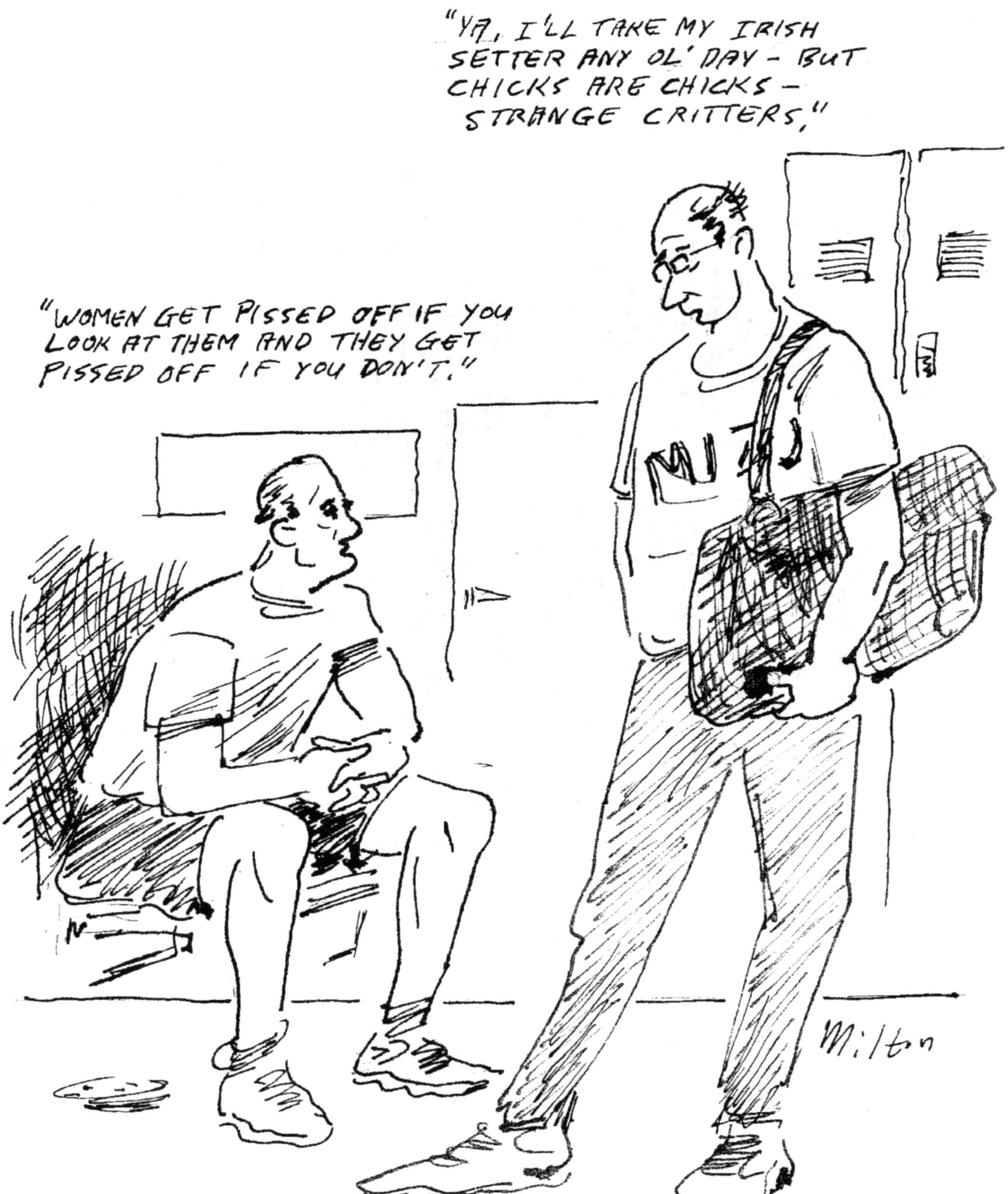
"YA, I'LL TAKE MY IRISH SETTER ANY OL' DAY - BUT CHICKS ARE CHICKS - STRANGE CRITTERS."
"WOMEN GET PISSED OFF IF YOU LOOK AT THEM AND THEY GET PISSED OFF IF YOU DON'T."
Milton

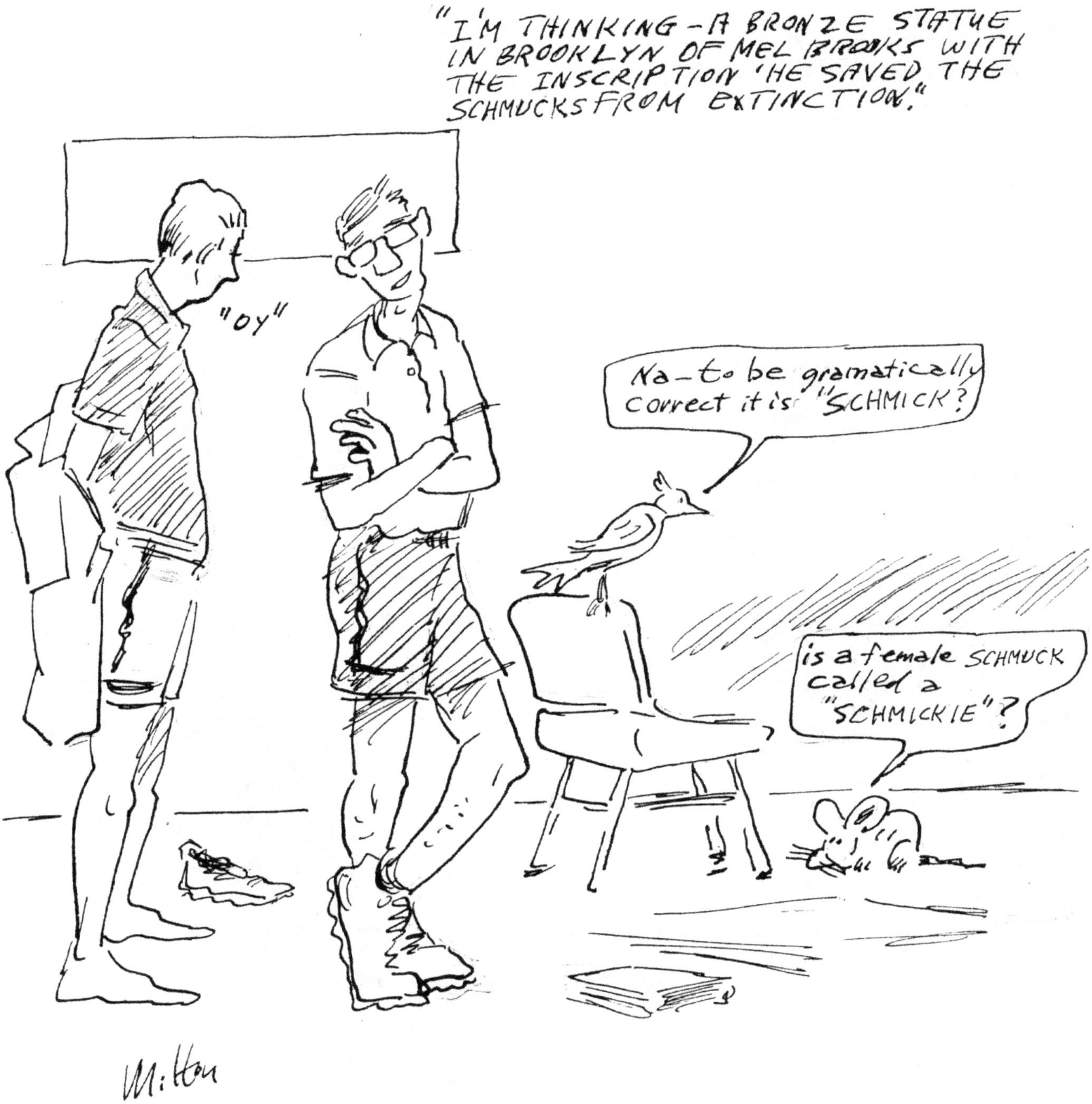
"I'M THINKING - A BRONZE STATUE IN BROOKLYN OF MEL BROOKS WITH THE INSCRIPTION 'HE SAVED THE SCHMUCKS FROM EXTINCTION."
"OY"
Na - to be gramatically correct it is "SCHMICK?
is a female SCHMUCK called a "SCHMICKIE"?
Milton

I'M GOING TO START USING THE WOMEN'S LOCKER ROOM - THAT WAY I'LL BE AVOIDING ALL THE GAYS.. AT LEAST THEN I'LL KNOW WHAT I'M DEALING WITH....

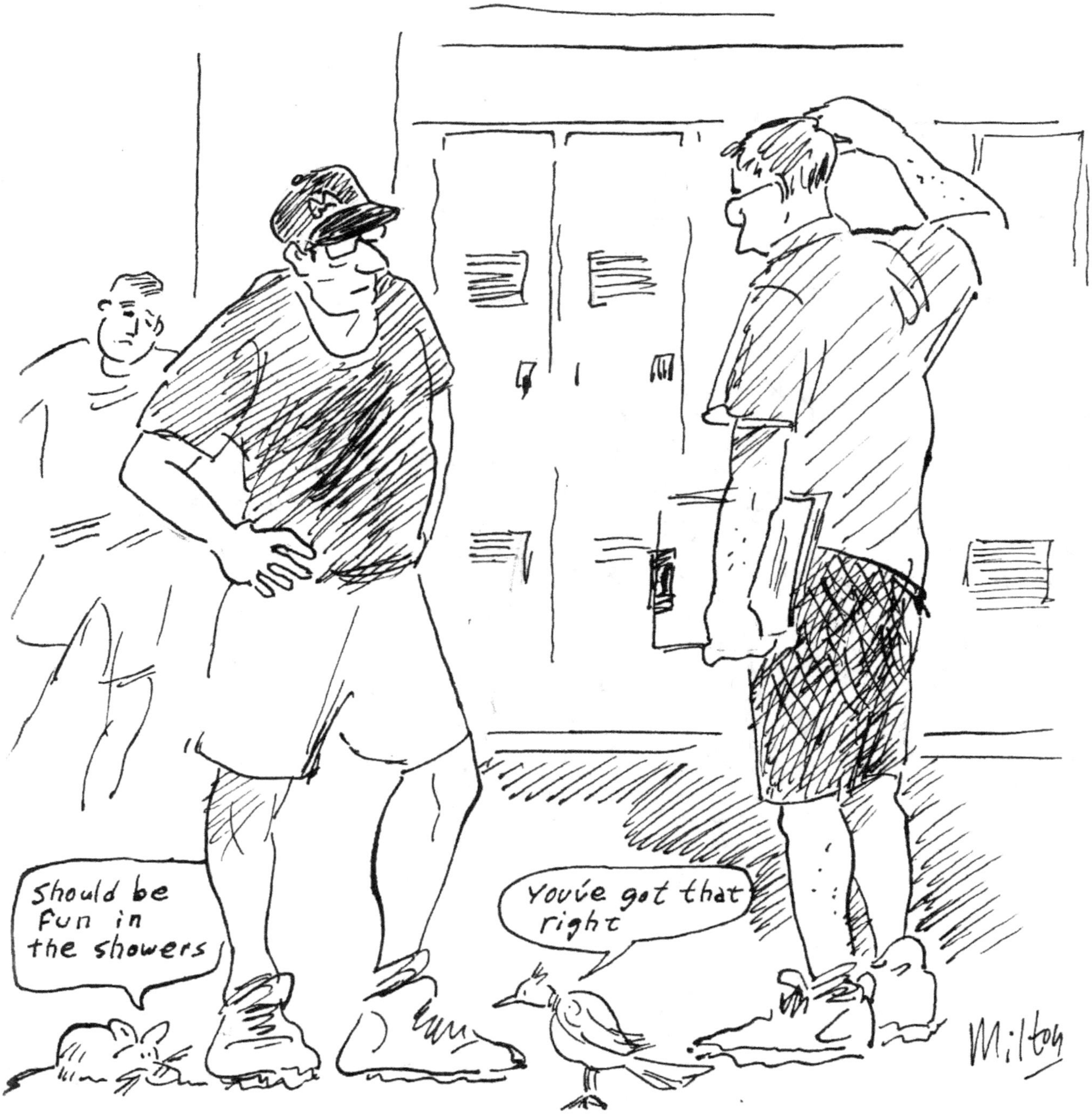
Should be fun in the showers
You've got that right
Milton

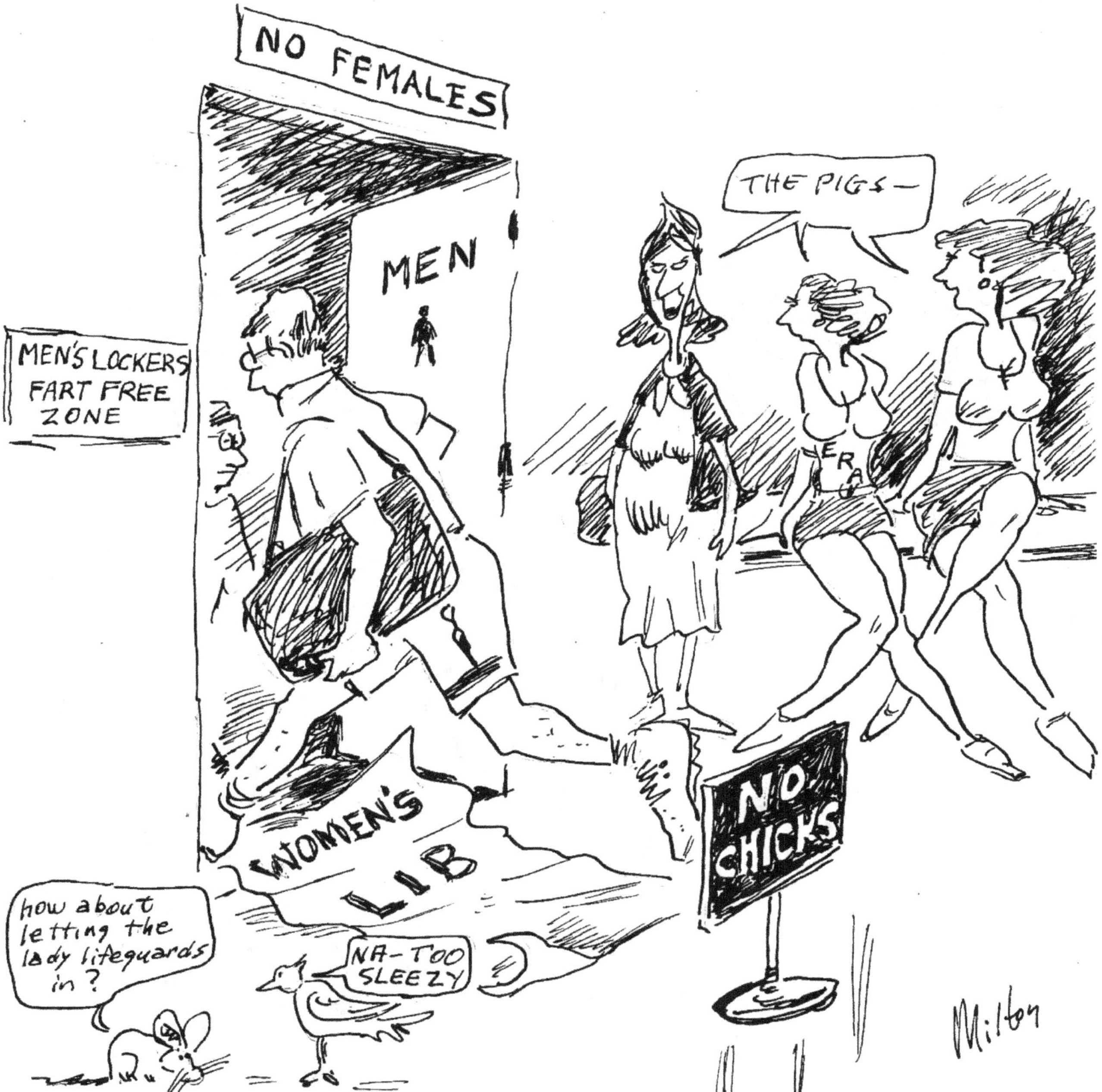
NO FEMALES
MEN
MEN'S LOCKERS FART FREE ZONE
THE PIGS—
ERA
WOMEN'S LIB
NO CHICKS
how about letting the lady lifeguards in?
NA-TOO SLEEZY
Milton

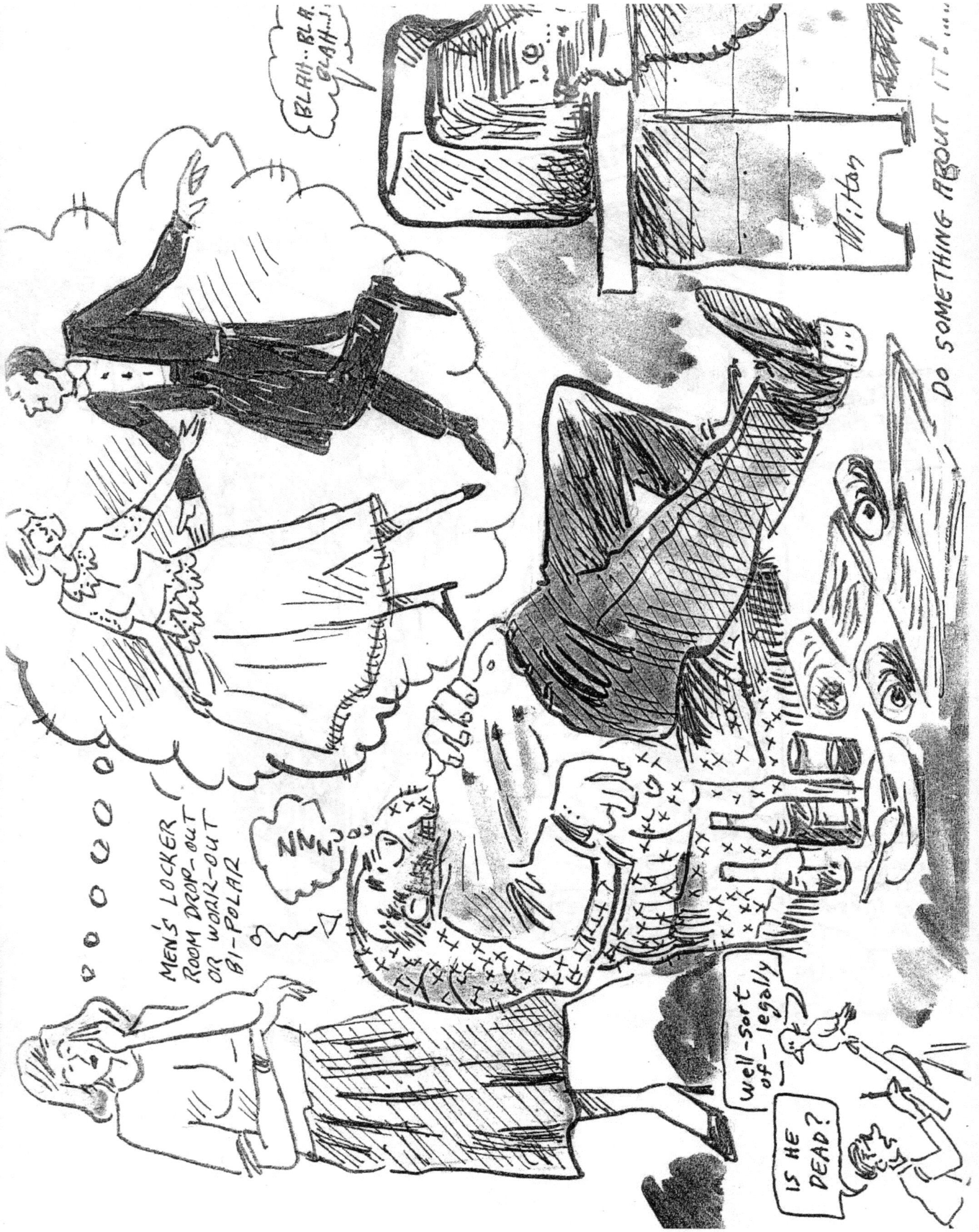
MEN'S LOCKER ROOM DROP-OUT OR WORK-OUT BI-POLAR
NNN
BLAH.. BLA. BLAH...!
IS HE DEAD?
Well-sort of-legally
DO SOMETHING ABOUT IT!....

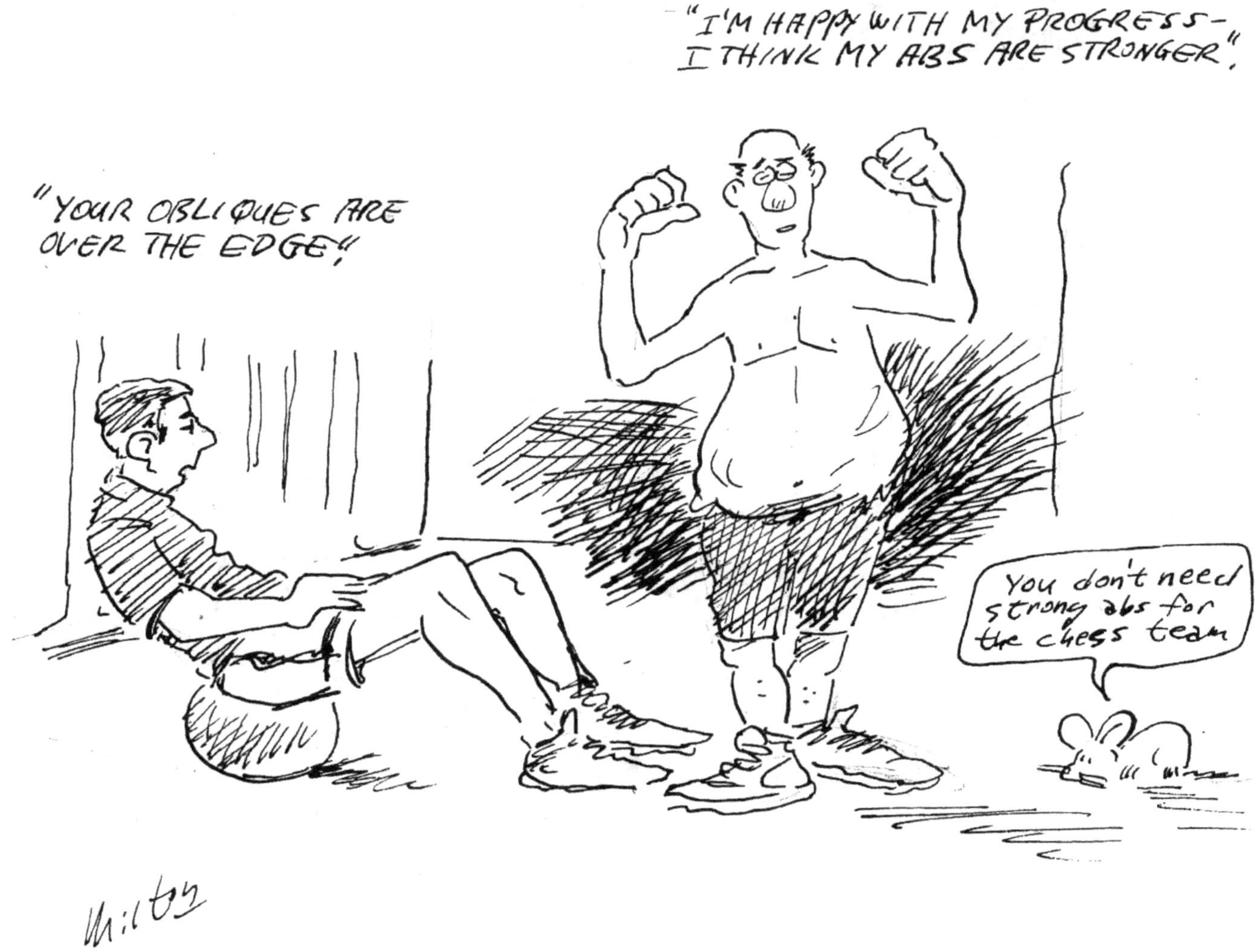
"I'M HAPPY WITH MY PROGRESS-
I THINK MY ABS ARE STRONGER".
"YOUR OBLIQUES ARE
OVER THE EDGE!"
You don't need
strong abs for
the chess team
Milton

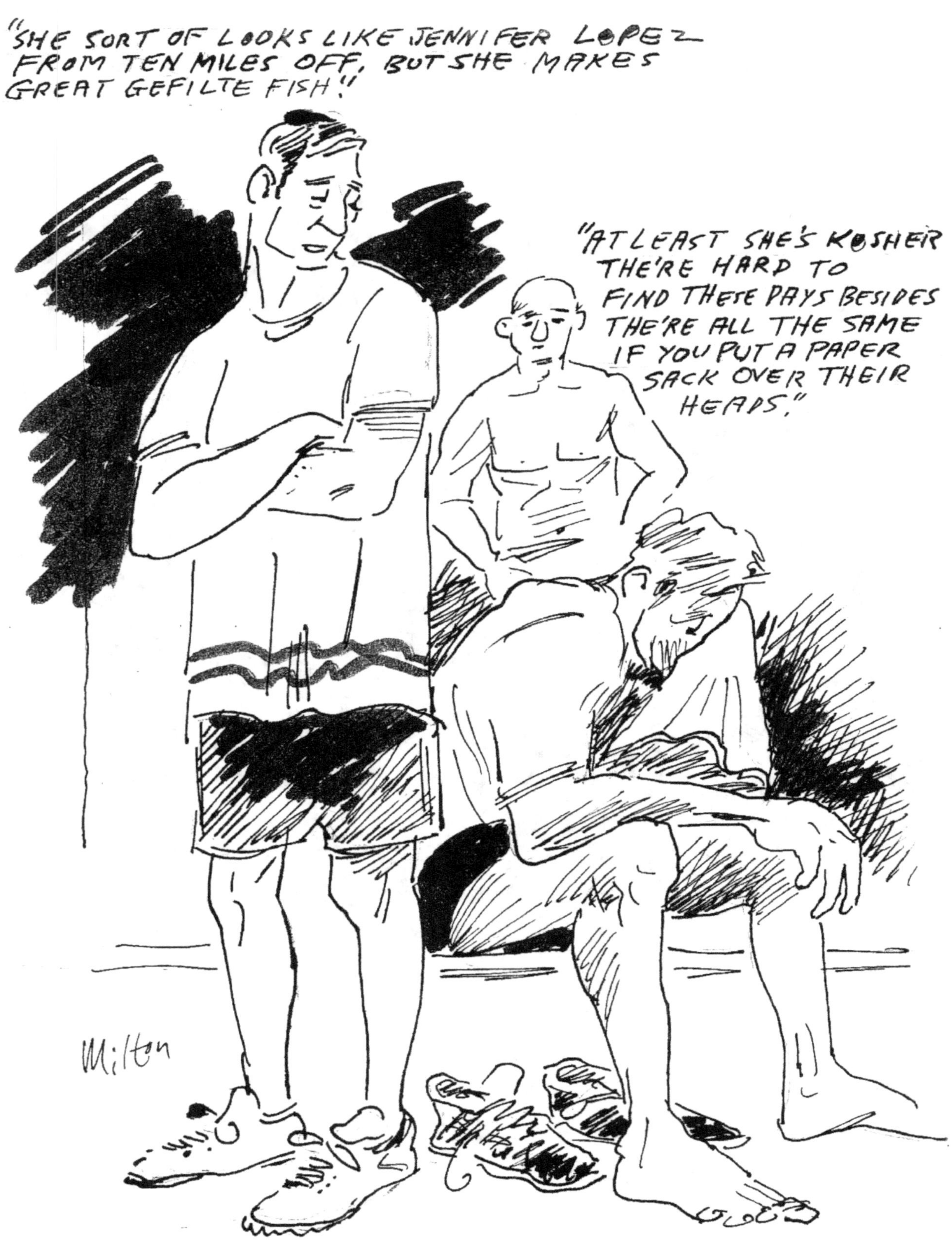
"SHE SORT OF LOOKS LIKE JENNIFER LOPEZ FROM TEN MILES OFF, BUT SHE MAKES GREAT GEFILTE FISH!"
"AT LEAST SHE'S KOSHER THE'RE HARD TO FIND THESE DAYS BESIDES THE'RE ALL THE SAME IF YOU PUT A PAPER SACK OVER THEIR HEADS."
Milton

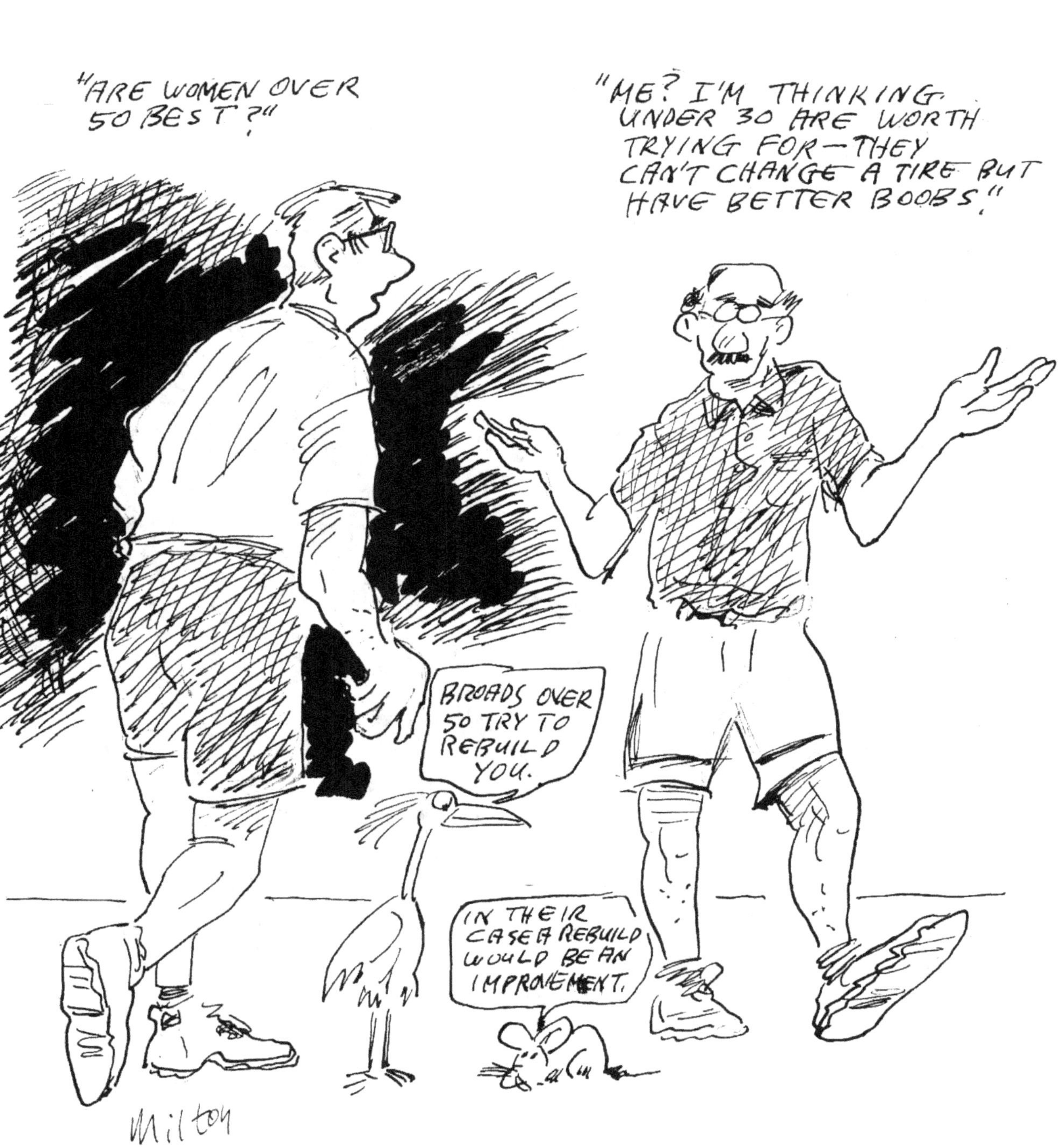
"ARE WOMEN OVER 50 BEST?"
"ME? I'M THINKING UNDER 30 ARE WORTH TRYING FOR—THEY CAN'T CHANGE A TIRE BUT HAVE BETTER BOOBS."
BROADS OVER 50 TRY TO REBUILD YOU.
IN THEIR CASE A REBUILD WOULD BE AN IMPROVEMENT.
Milton

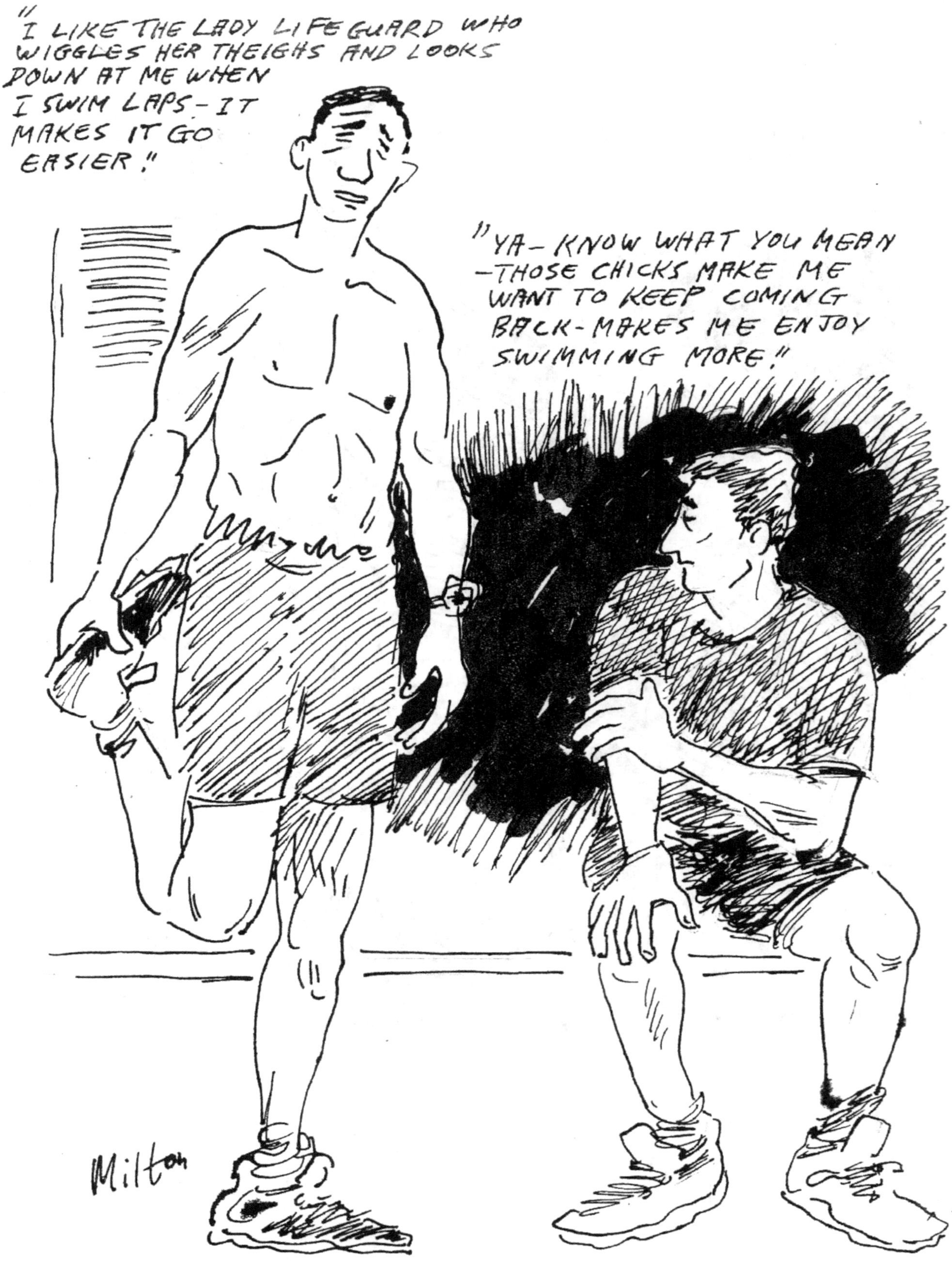
"I LIKE THE LADY LIFEGUARD WHO WIGGLES HER THEIGHS AND LOOKS DOWN AT ME WHEN I SWIM LAPS - IT MAKES IT GO EASIER!"
"YA - KNOW WHAT YOU MEAN - THOSE CHICKS MAKE ME WANT TO KEEP COMING BACK - MAKES ME ENJOY SWIMMING MORE!"
Milton

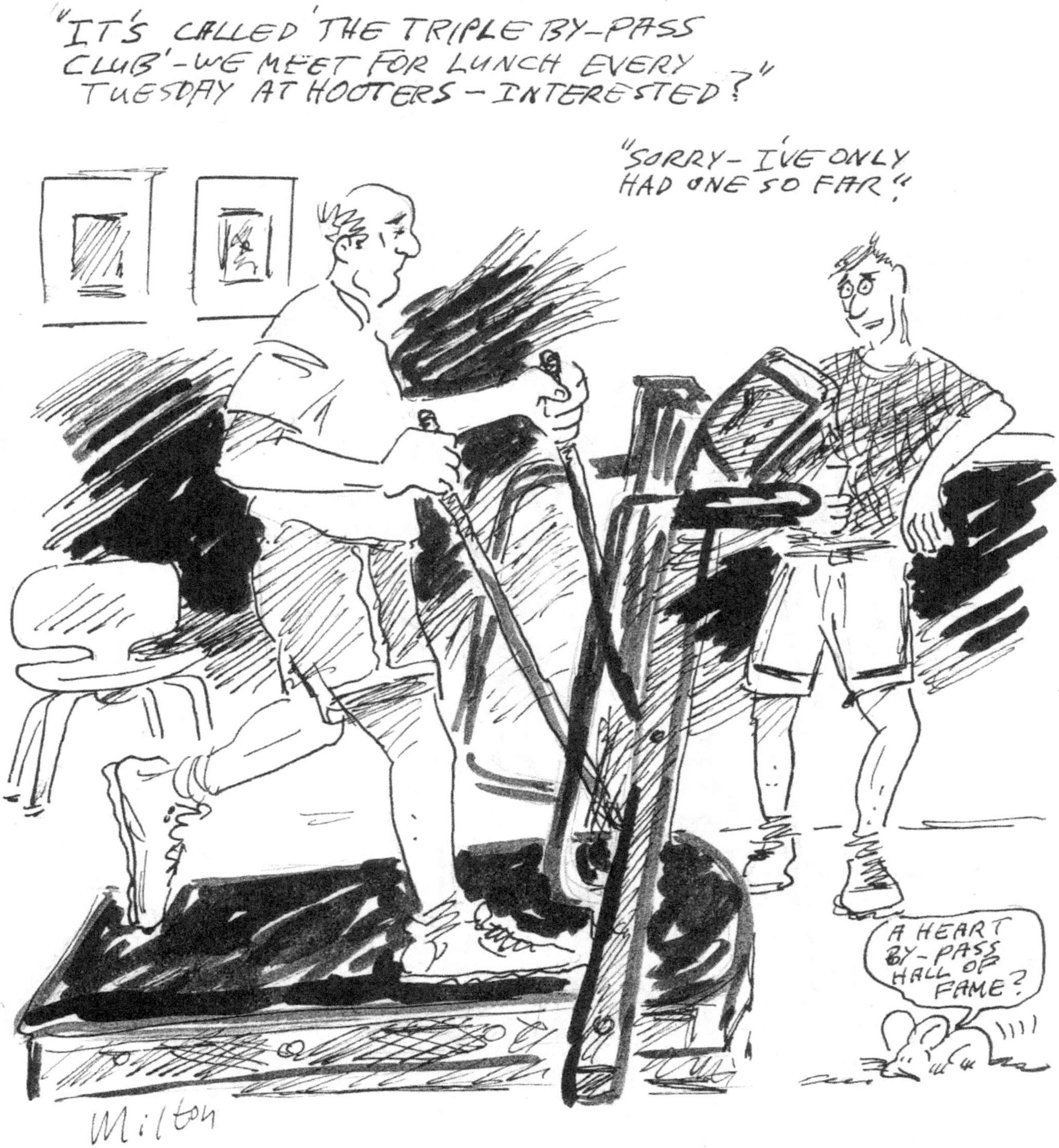
"IT'S CALLED 'THE TRIPLE BY-PASS CLUB'-WE MEET FOR LUNCH EVERY TUESDAY AT HOOTERS - INTERESTED?"
"SORRY- I'VE ONLY HAD ONE SO FAR!"
A HEART BY-PASS HALL OF FAME?
Milton

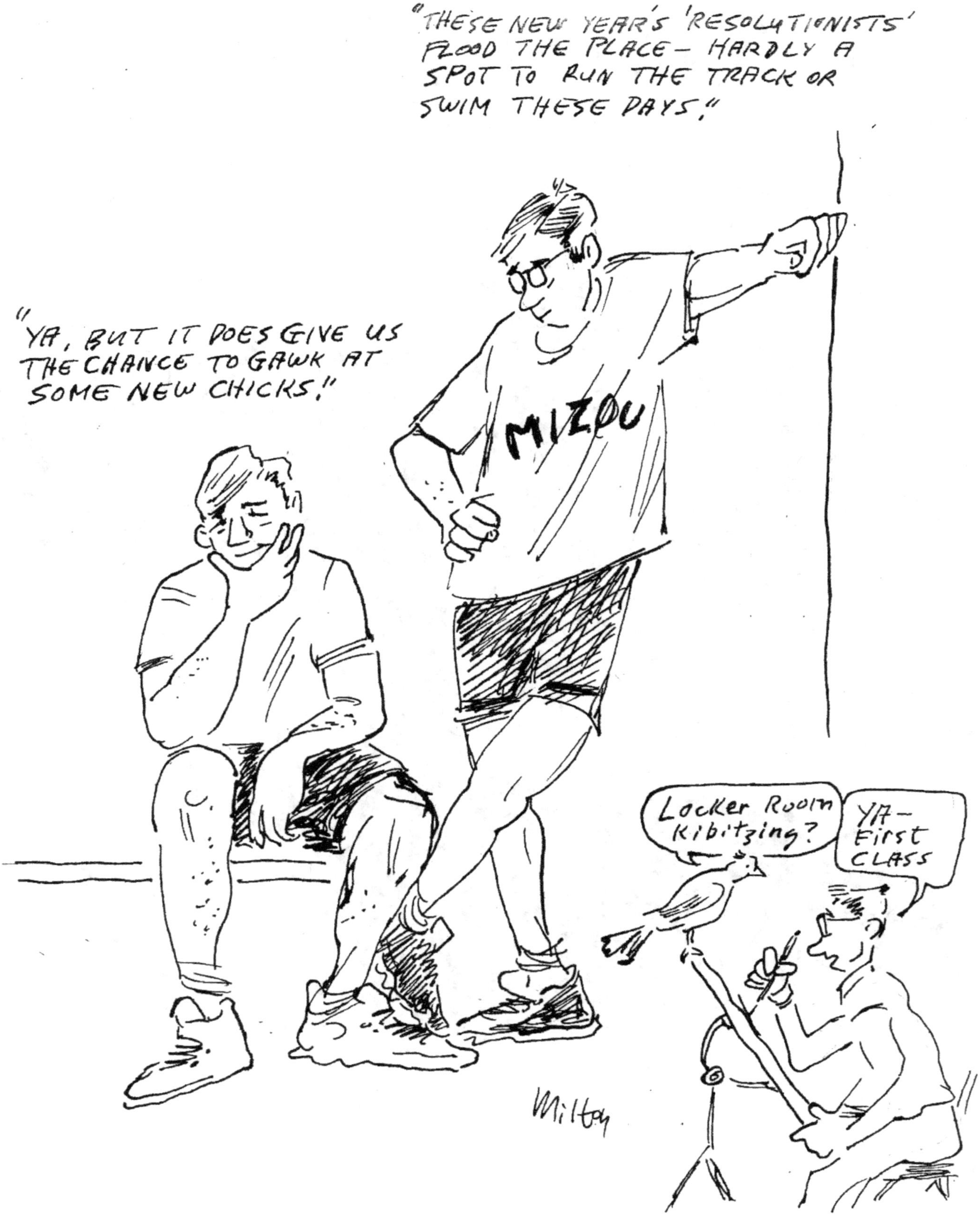
"THESE NEW YEAR'S 'RESOLUTIONISTS' FLOOD THE PLACE— HARDLY A SPOT TO RUN THE TRACK OR SWIM THESE DAYS!"
"YA, BUT IT DOES GIVE US THE CHANCE TO GAWK AT SOME NEW CHICKS!"
MIZOU
Locker Room Kibitzing?
YA— First CLASS
Milton

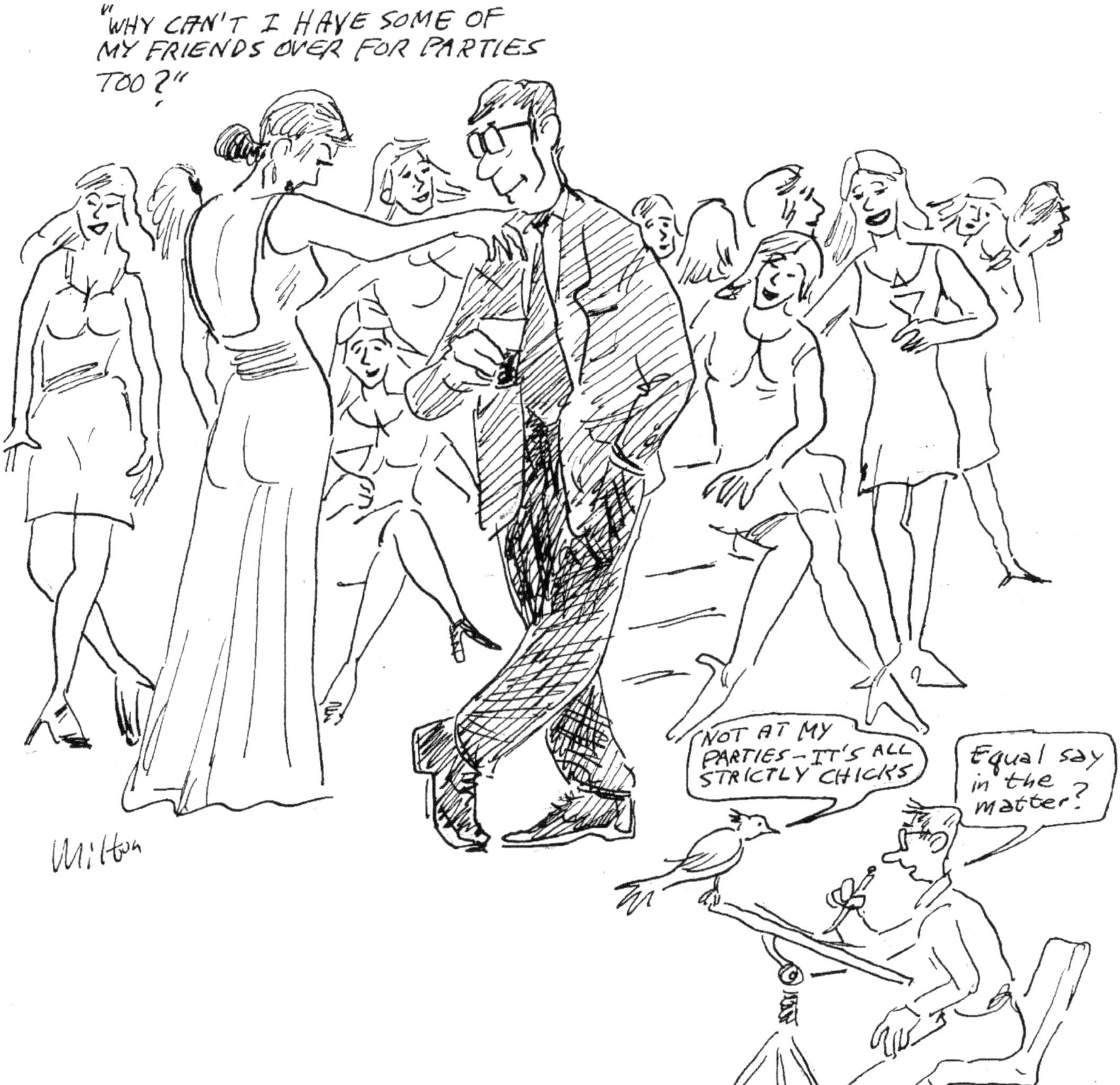
"WHY CAN'T I HAVE SOME OF MY FRIENDS OVER FOR PARTIES TOO?"
NOT AT MY PARTIES—IT'S ALL STRICTLY CHICKS
Equal say in the matter?
Milton

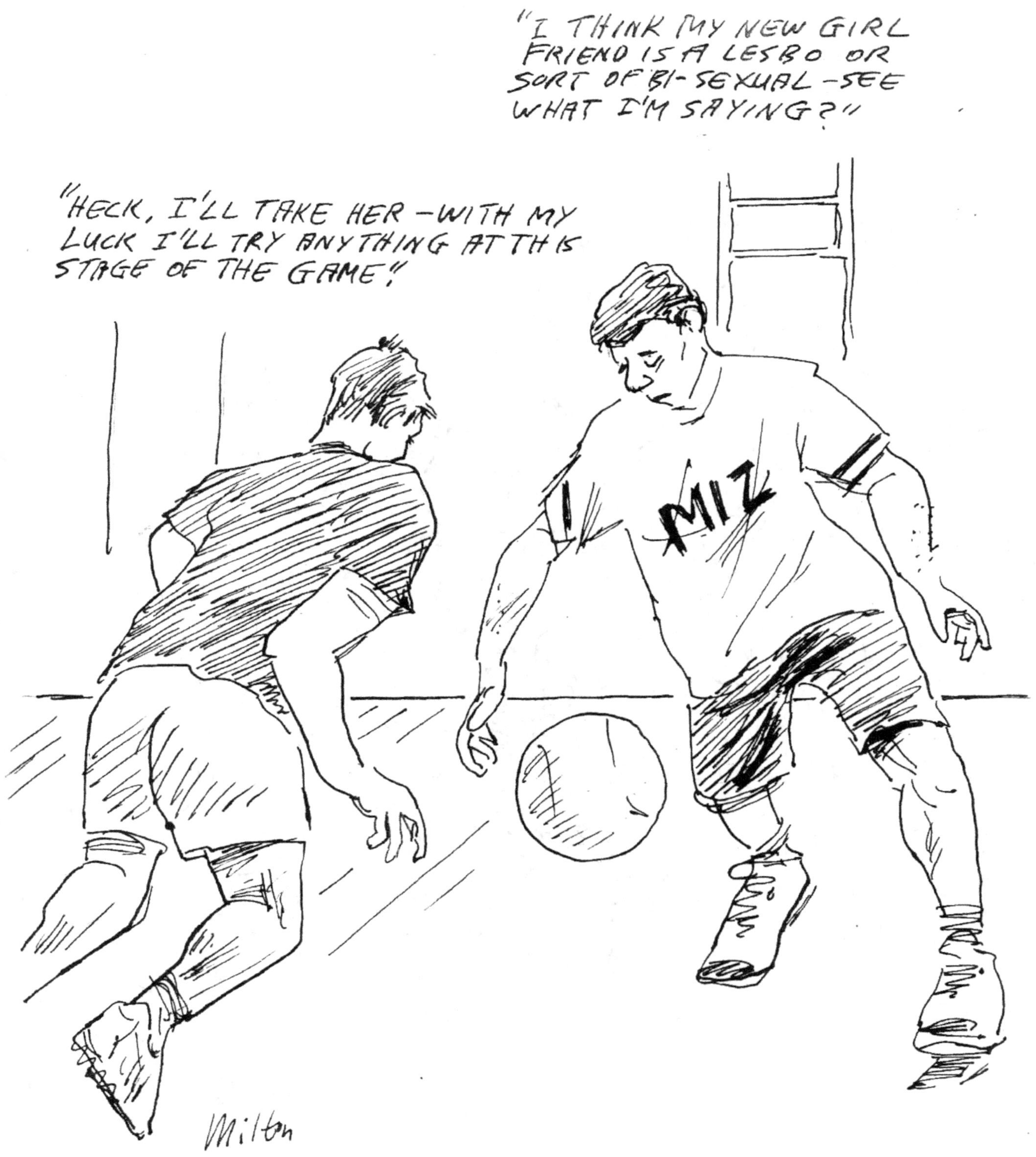
"I THINK MY NEW GIRL FRIEND IS A LESBO OR SORT OF BI-SEXUAL - SEE WHAT I'M SAYING?"
"HECK, I'LL TAKE HER - WITH MY LUCK I'LL TRY ANYTHING AT THIS STAGE OF THE GAME!"
MIZ
Milton

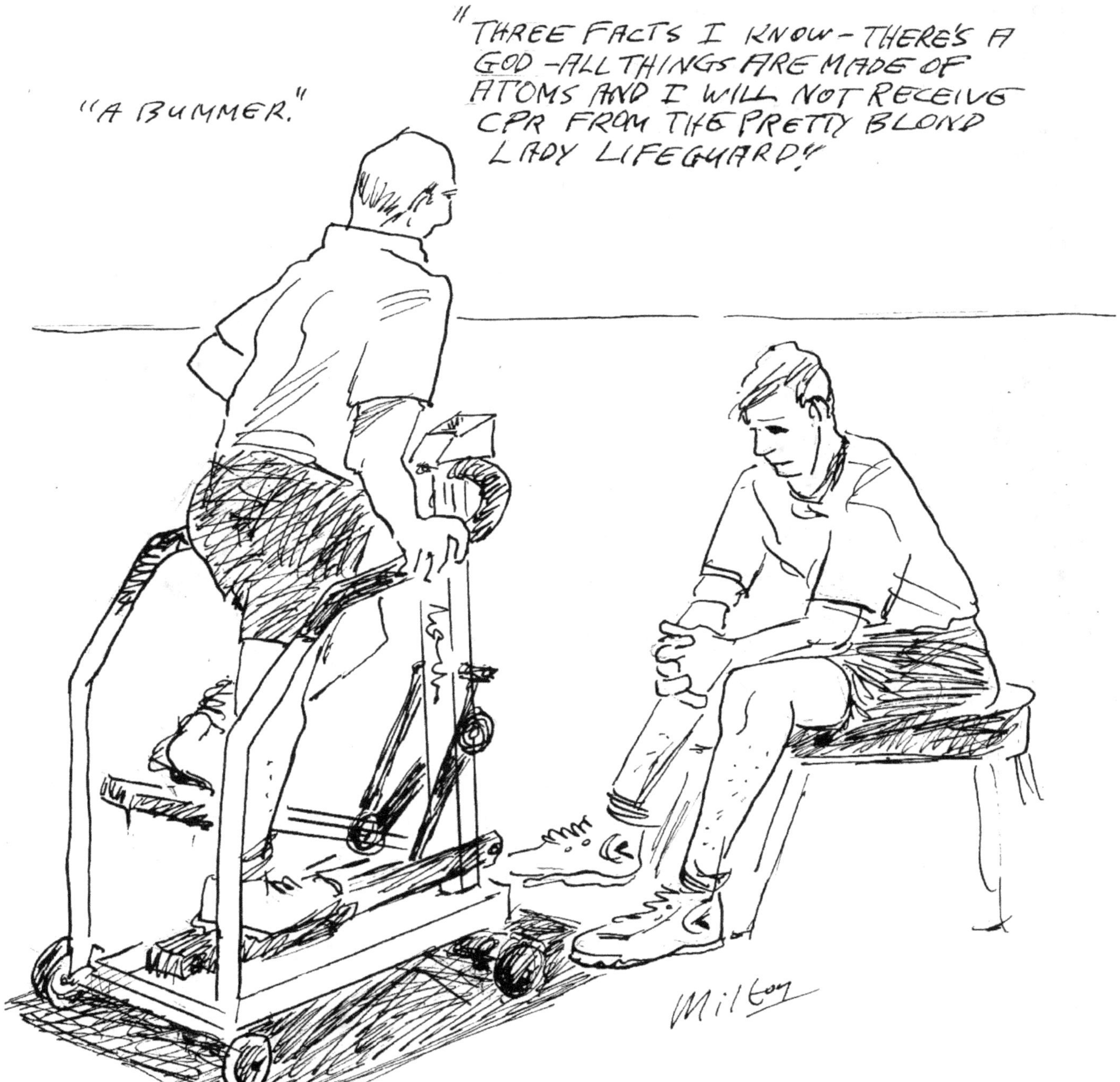
"A BUMMER."
"THREE FACTS I KNOW - THERE'S A GOD - ALL THINGS ARE MADE OF ATOMS AND I WILL NOT RECEIVE CPR FROM THE PRETTY BLOND LADY LIFEGUARD!"
Milton

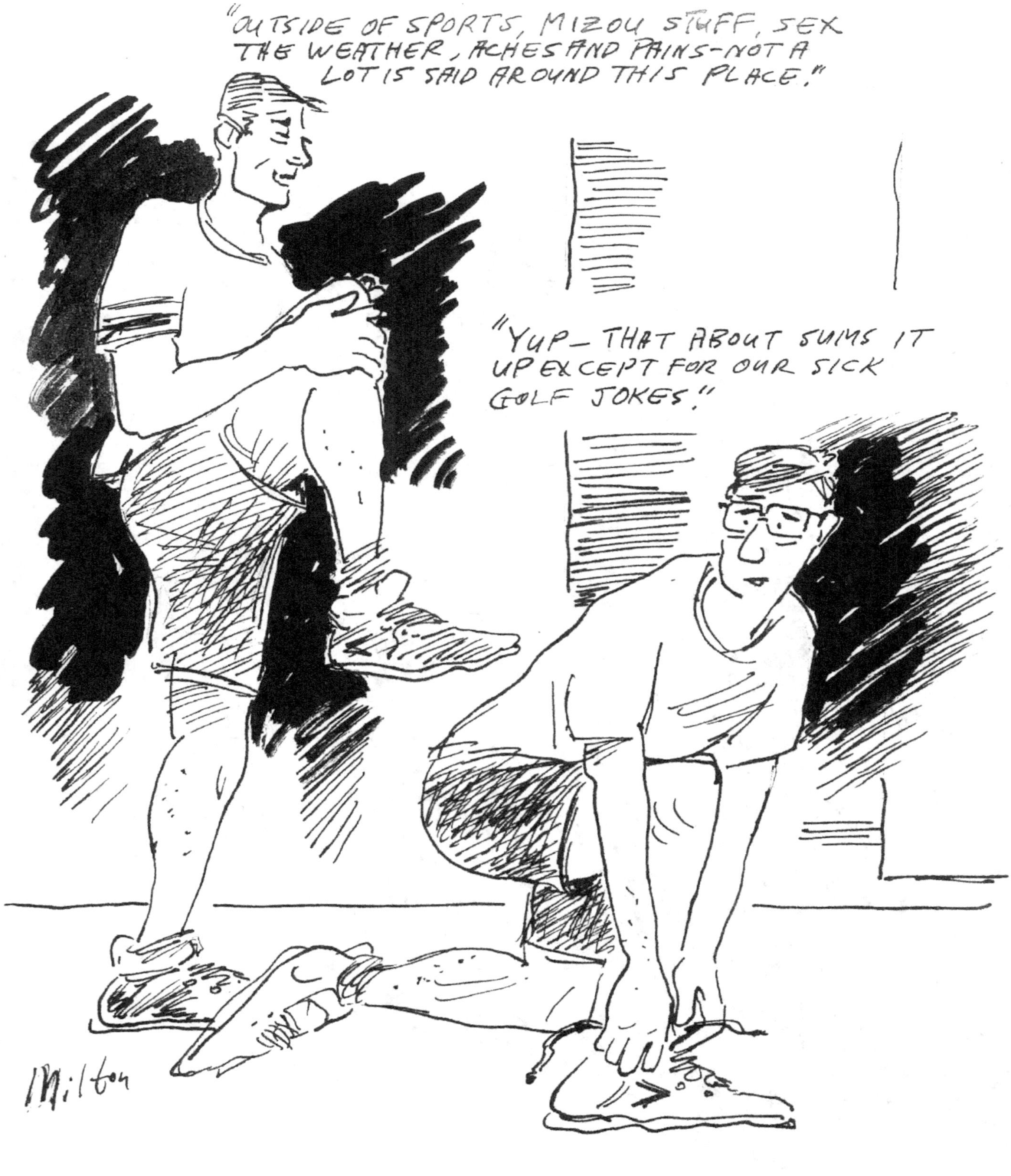
"OUTSIDE OF SPORTS, MIZOU STUFF, SEX
THE WEATHER, ACHES AND PAINS-NOT A
LOT IS SAID AROUND THIS PLACE!"
"YUP-THAT ABOUT SUMS IT
UP EXCEPT FOR OUR SICK
GOLF JOKES!"
Milton

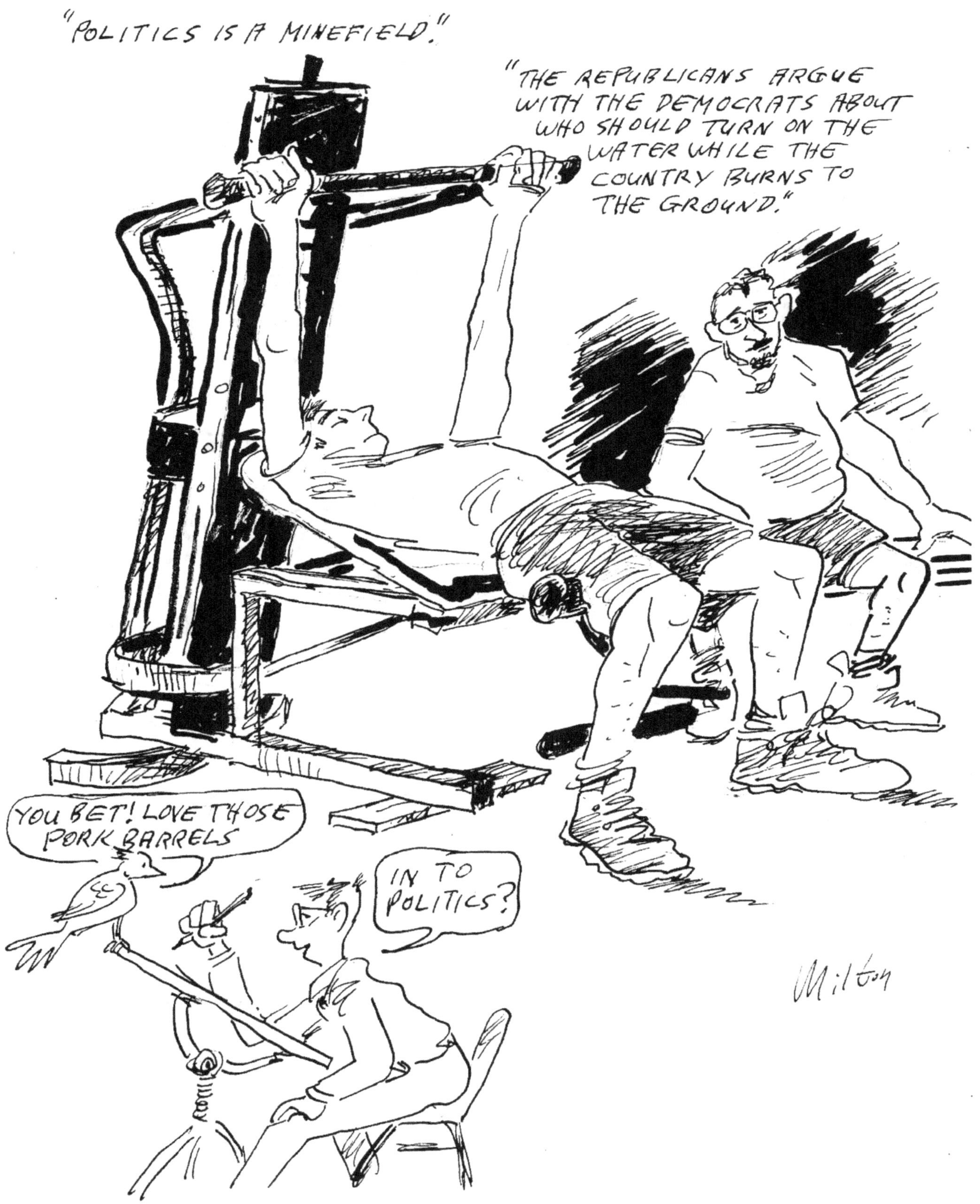
"POLITICS IS A MINEFIELD."
"THE REPUBLICANS ARGUE WITH THE DEMOCRATS ABOUT WHO SHOULD TURN ON THE WATER WHILE THE COUNTRY BURNS TO THE GROUND."
YOU BET! LOVE THOSE PORK BARRELS
IN TO POLITICS?
Milton

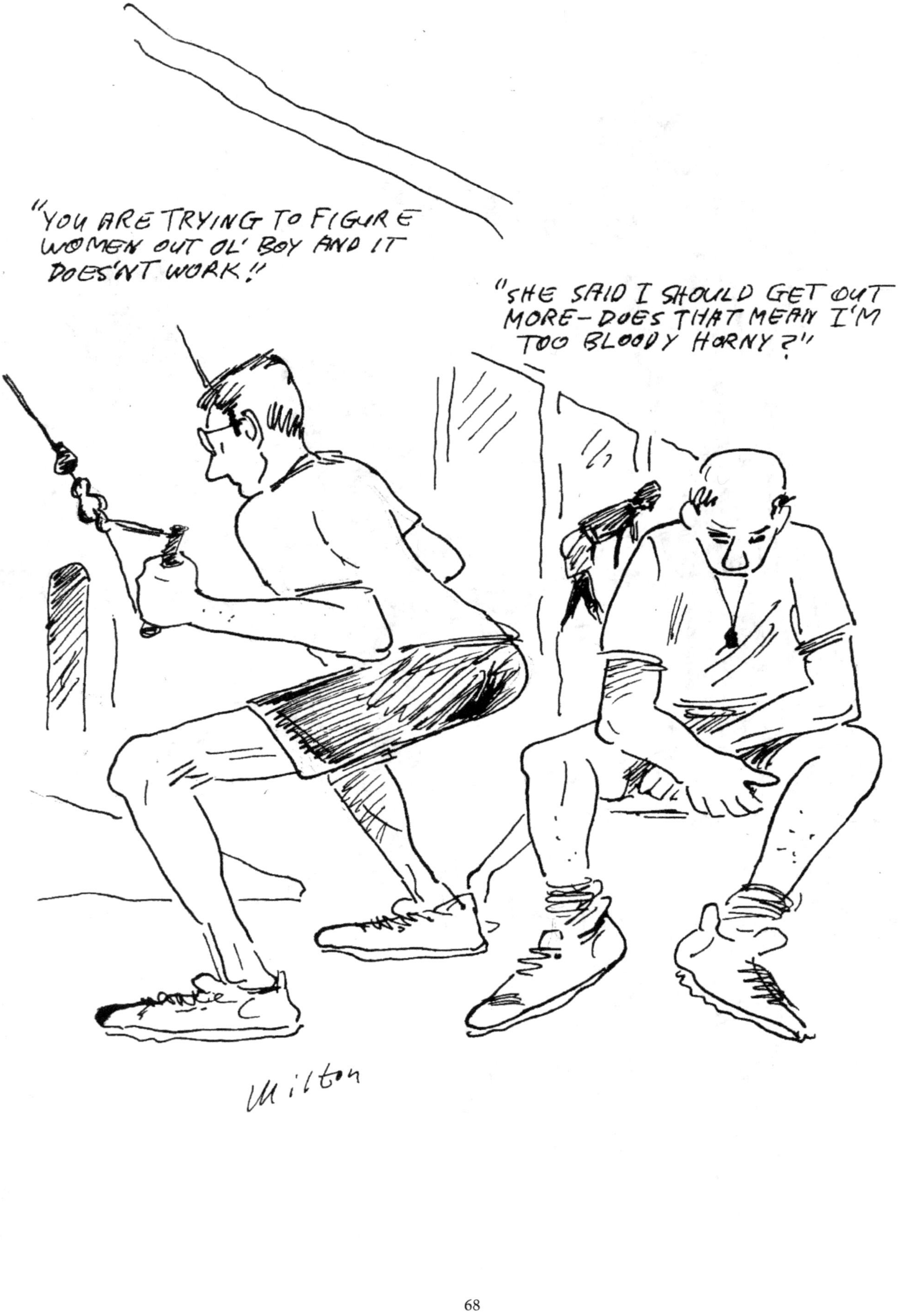
"YOU ARE TRYING TO FIGURE WOMEN OUT OL' BOY AND IT DOES'NT WORK!"
"SHE SAID I SHOULD GET OUT MORE– DOES THAT MEAN I'M TOO BLOODY HORNY?"
Milton

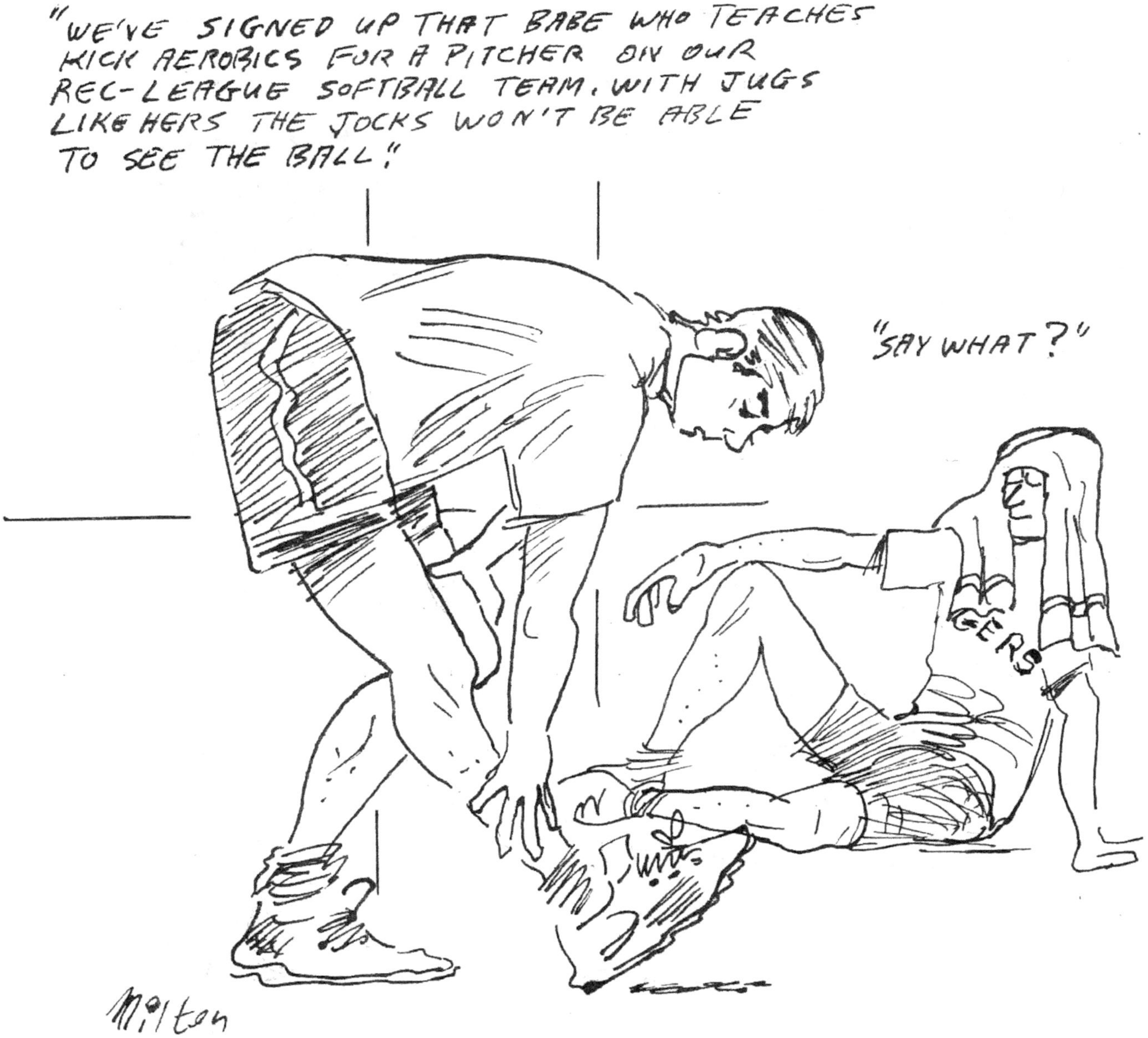
"WE'VE SIGNED UP THAT BABE WHO TEACHES KICK AEROBICS FOR A PITCHER ON OUR REC-LEAGUE SOFTBALL TEAM. WITH JUGS LIKE HERS THE JOCKS WON'T BE ABLE TO SEE THE BALL!"
"SAY WHAT?"
GERS
Milton

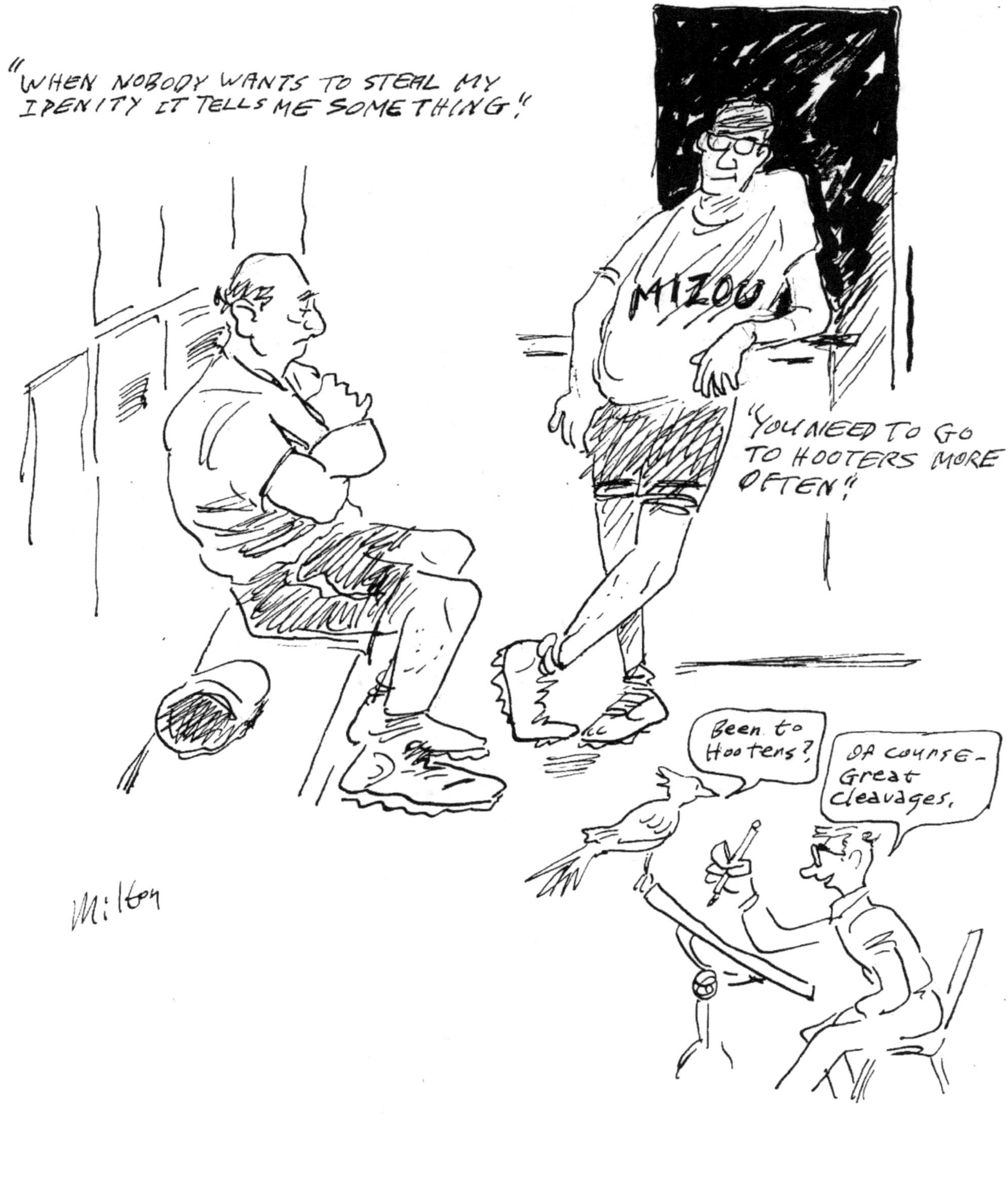
"WHEN NOBODY WANTS TO STEAL MY IDENITY IT TELLS ME SOMETHING!"
MIZOU
"YOU NEED TO GO TO HOOTERS MORE OFTEN!"
Been to Hootens?
Of counse-Great cleavages.
Milton

AQUATICS ECONOMICS 101
SWIMMING POOL DILEMA
LIFEGUARD SUPPLY AND DEMAND....

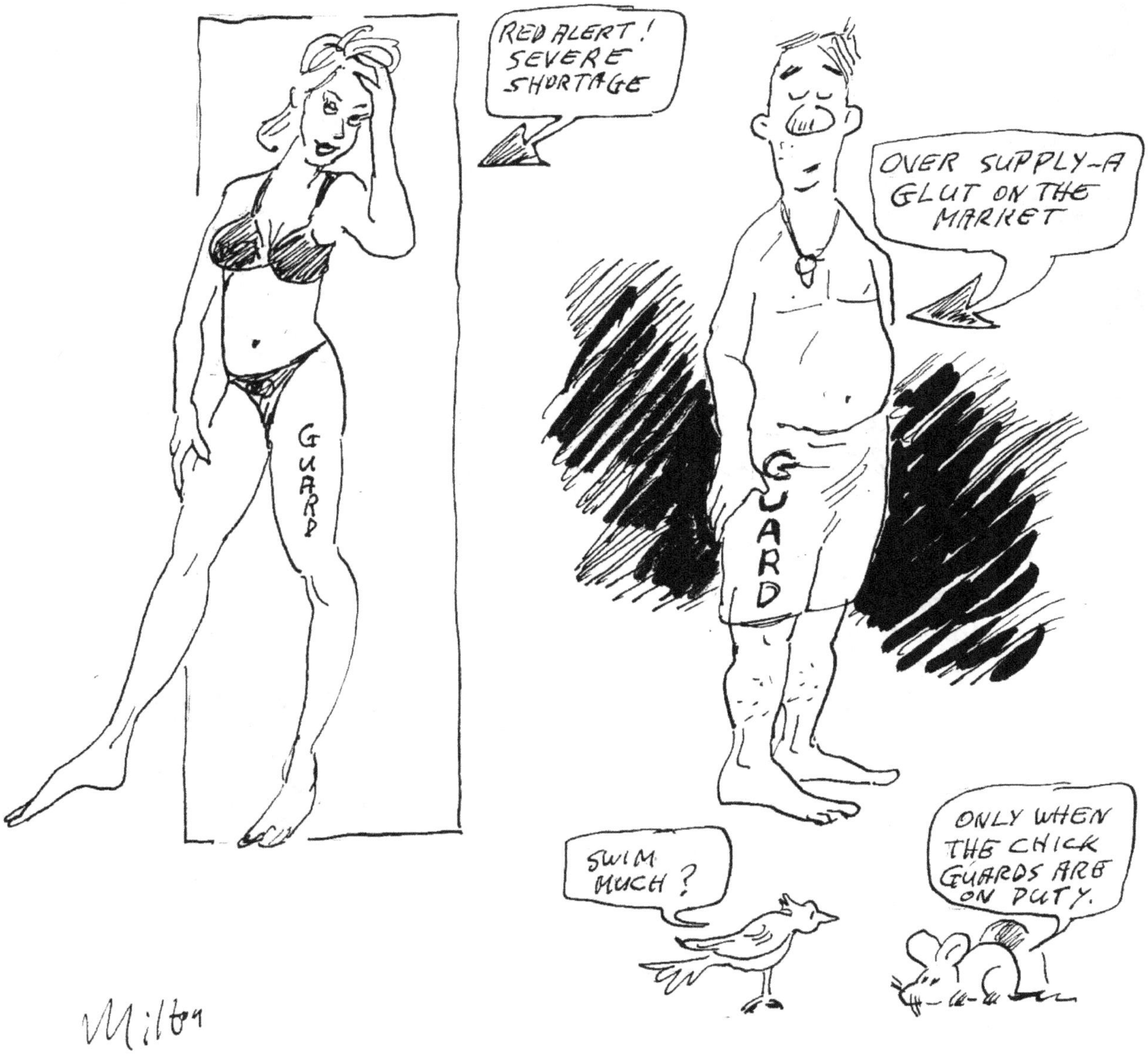
RED ALERT! SEVERE SHORTAGE
GUARD
OVER SUPPLY-A GLUT ON THE MARKET
GUARD
SWIM MUCH?
ONLY WHEN THE CHICK GUARDS ARE ON DUTY.
Milton

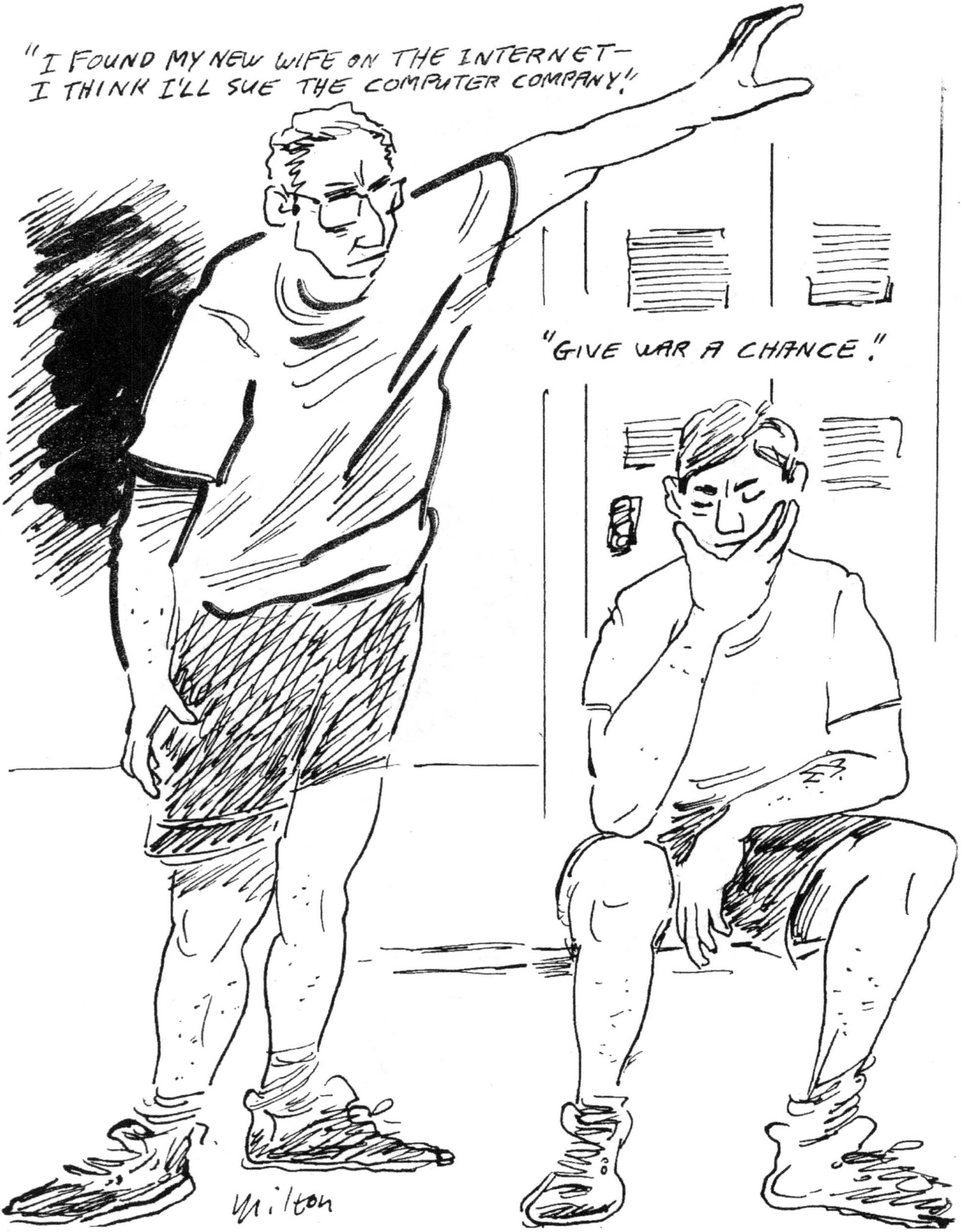
"I FOUND MY NEW WIFE ON THE INTERNET—
I THINK I'LL SUE THE COMPUTER COMPANY!"
"GIVE WAR A CHANCE!"
Milton

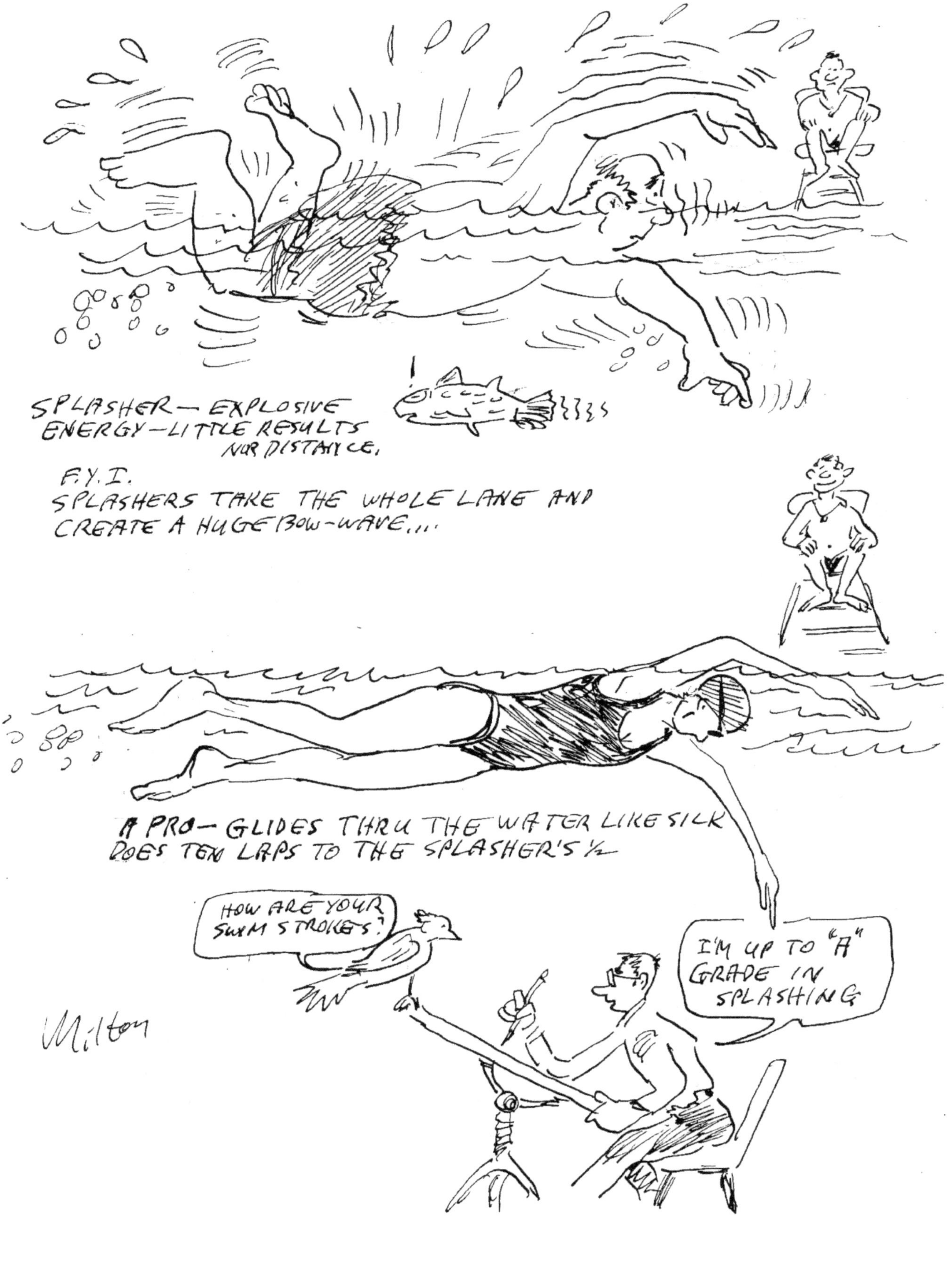
SPLASHER— EXPLOSIVE
ENERGY—LITTLE RESULTS
NOR DISTANCE.
F.Y.I.
SPLASHERS TAKE THE WHOLE LANE AND
CREATE A HUGE BOW-WAVE....
A PRO— GLIDES THRU THE WATER LIKE SILK
DOES TEN LAPS TO THE SPLASHER'S ½
HOW ARE YOUR SWIM STROKES?
I'M UP TO "A" GRADE IN SPLASHING
Milton

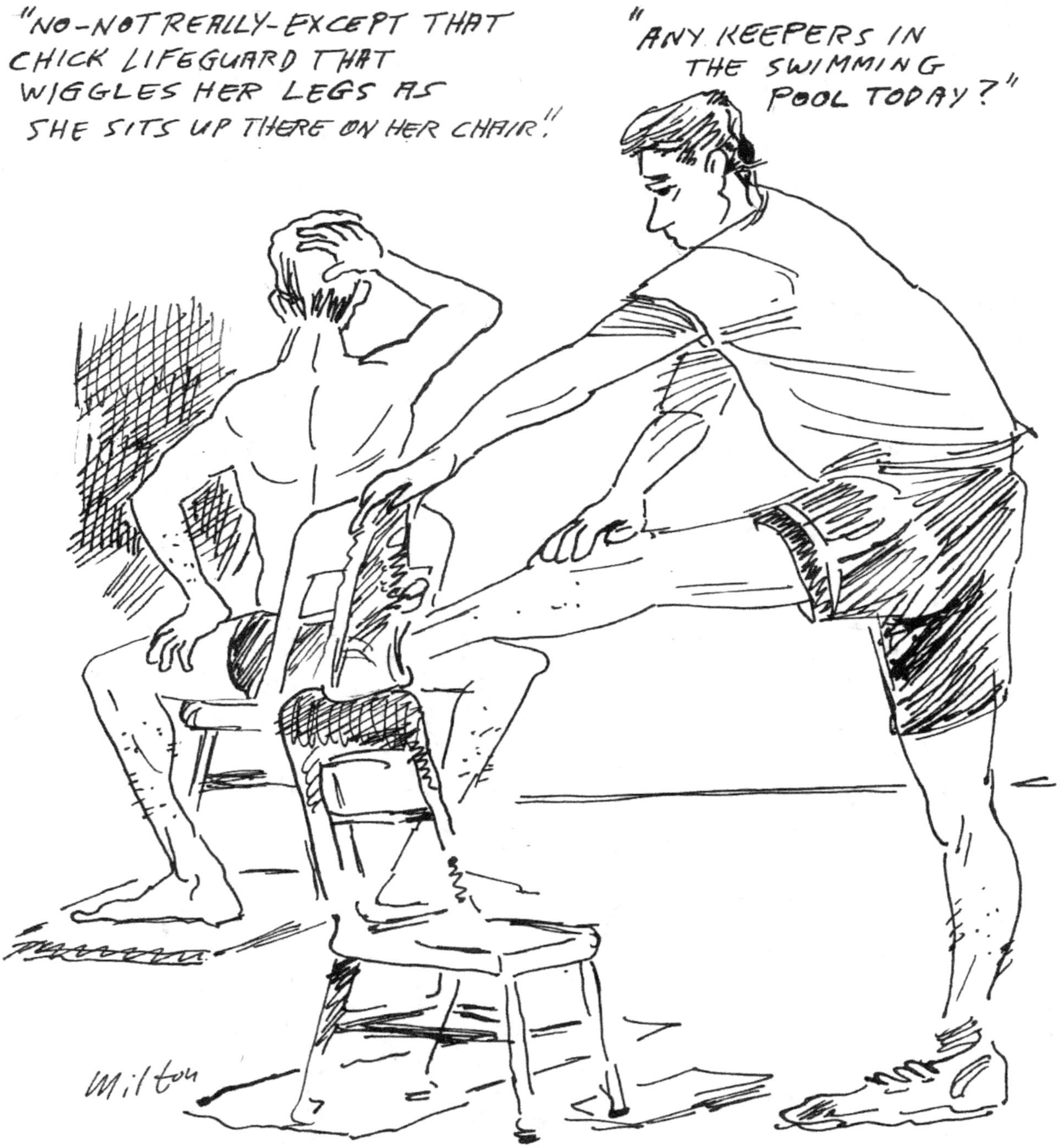
"NO-NOT REALLY-EXCEPT THAT CHICK LIFEGUARD THAT WIGGLES HER LEGS AS SHE SITS UP THERE ON HER CHAIR!"
"ANY KEEPERS IN THE SWIMMING POOL TODAY?"
Milton

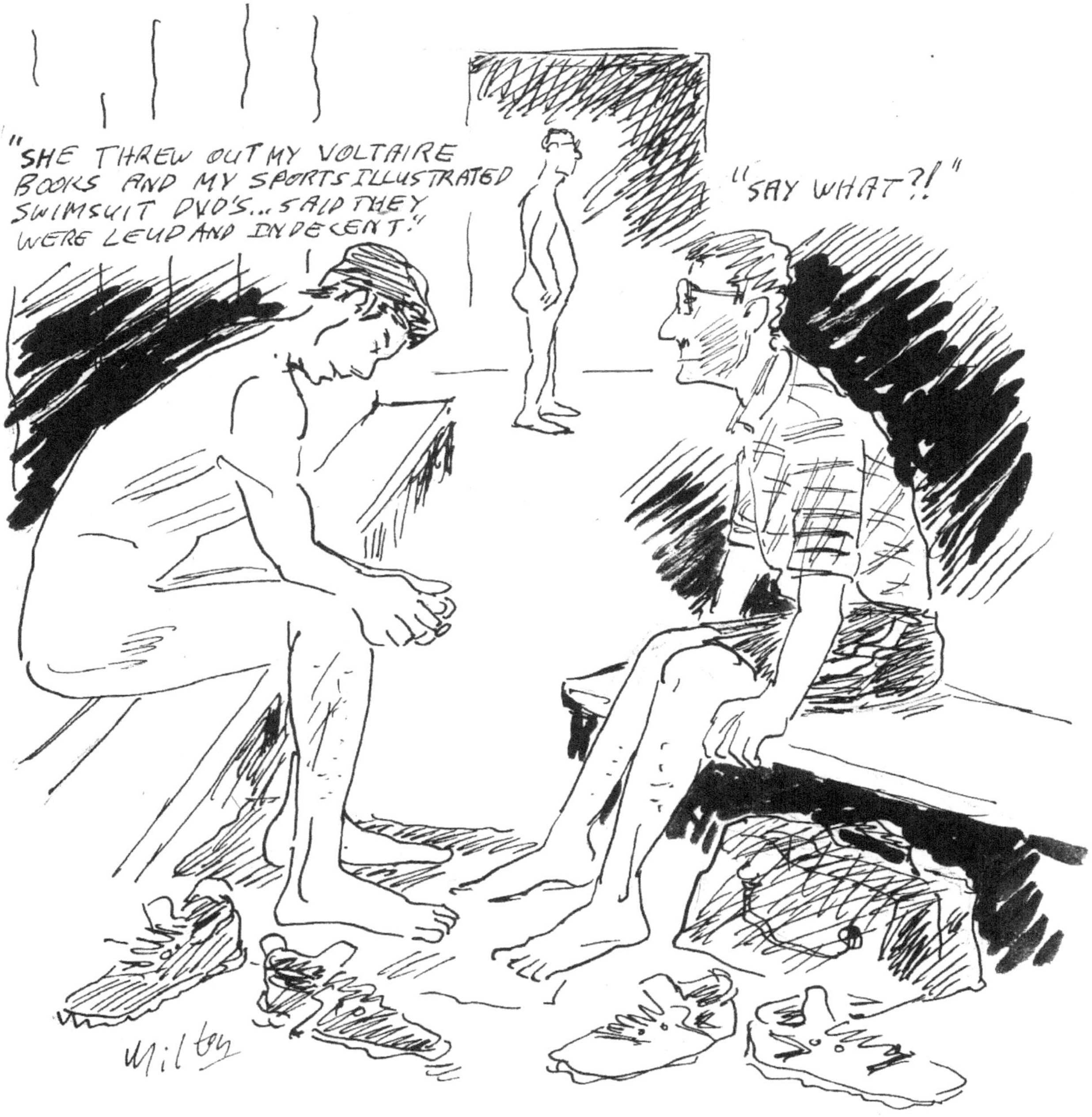
"SHE THREW OUT MY VOLTAIRE BOOKS AND MY SPORTS ILLUSTRATED SWIMSUIT DVD'S... SAID THEY WERE LEWD AND INDECENT."
"SAY WHAT?!"
Milton

"THIS PLACE HAS BEEN DECLARED THE SPERM BANK OF THE MID-WEST– SO MANY YOUNG HARD BALLS AROUND."

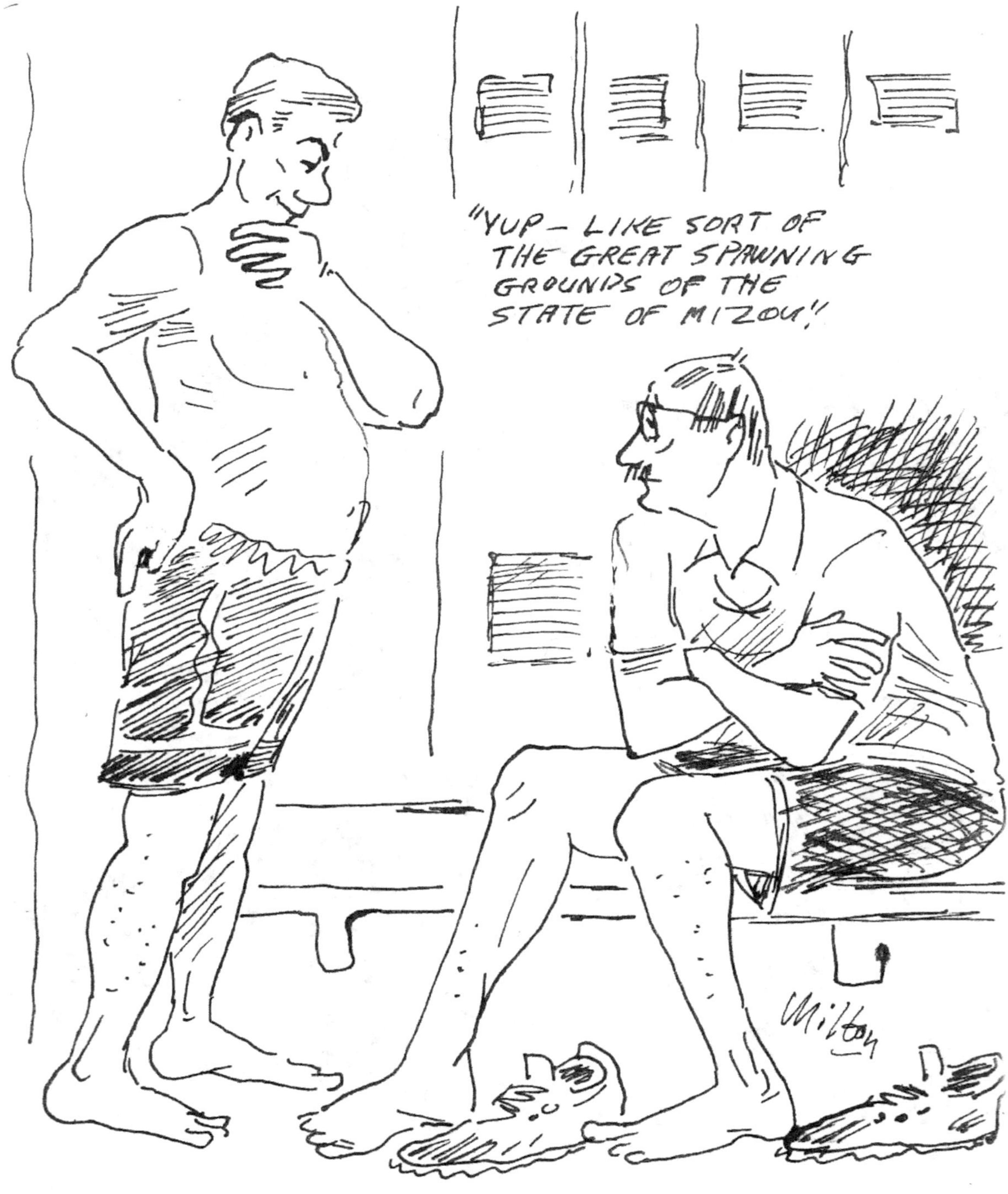
"YUP– LIKE SORT OF THE GREAT SPAWNING GROUNDS OF THE STATE OF MIZOU!"
Milton

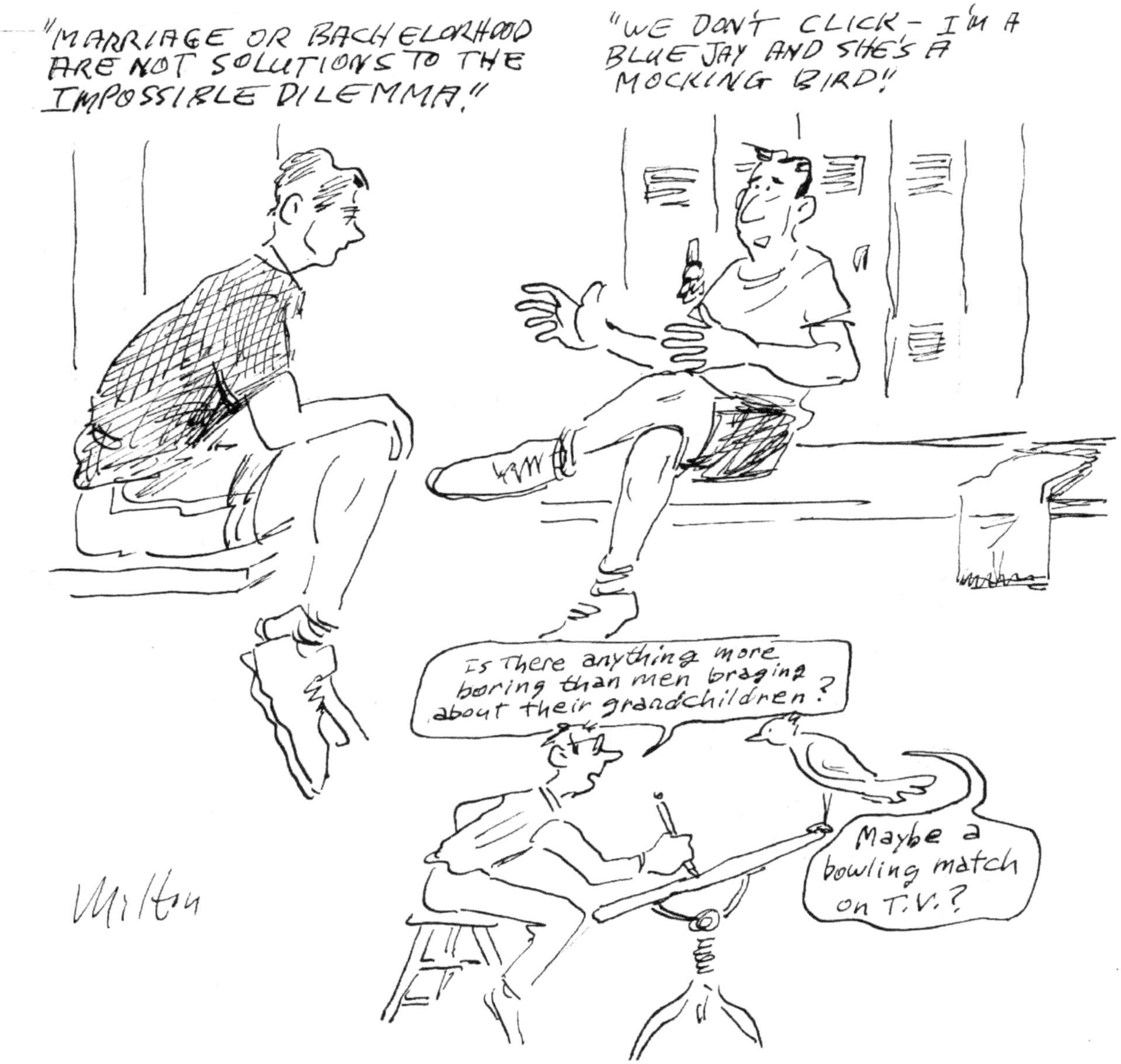
"MARRIAGE OR BACHELORHOOD ARE NOT SOLUTIONS TO THE IMPOSSIBLE DILEMMA."
"WE DON'T CLICK - I'M A BLUE JAY AND SHE'S A MOCKING BIRD!"
Is There anything more boring than men bragging about their grandchildren?
Maybe a bowling match on T.V.?
Milton

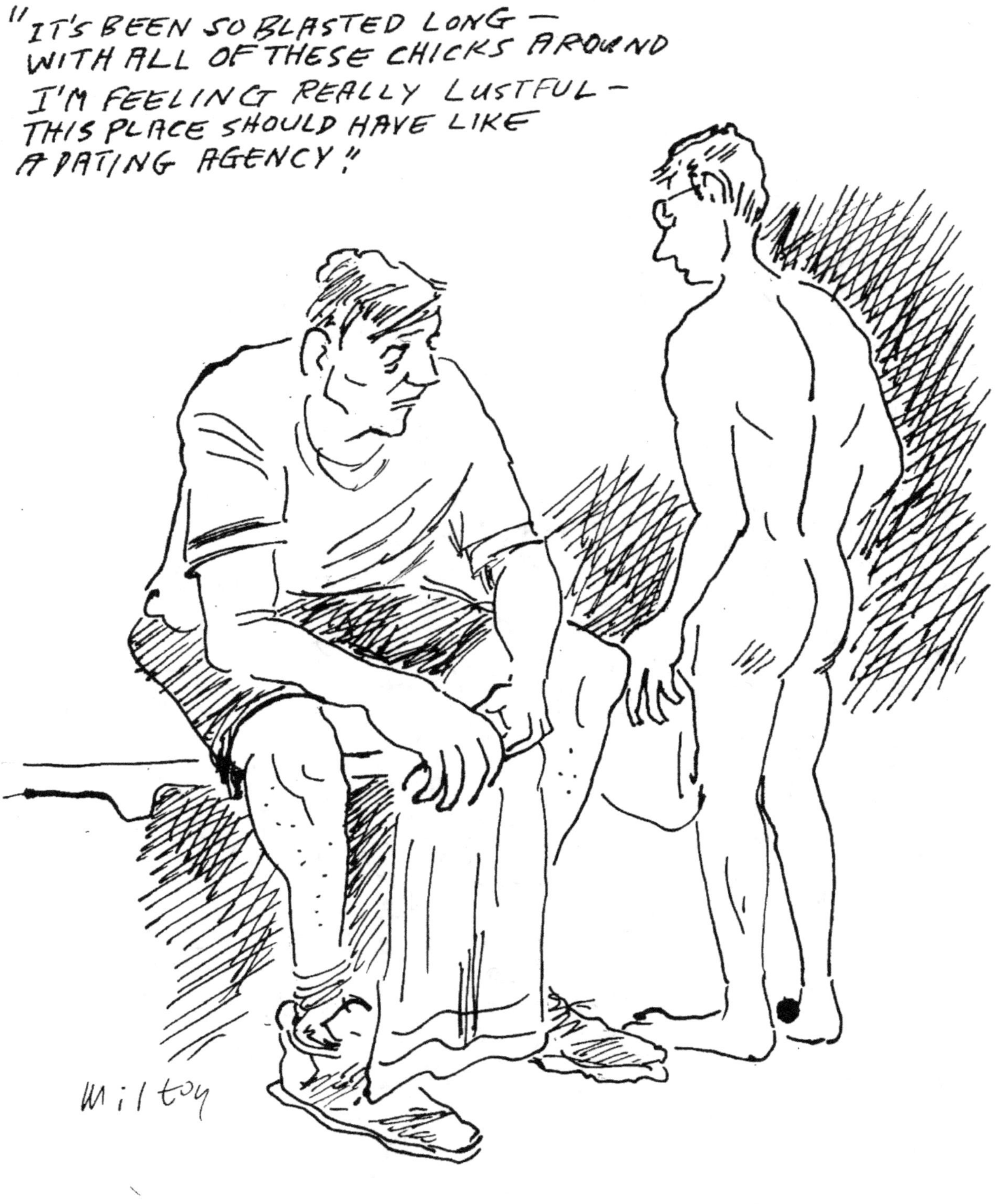
"IT'S BEEN SO BLASTED LONG — WITH ALL OF THESE CHICKS AROUND I'M FEELING REALLY LUSTFUL — THIS PLACE SHOULD HAVE LIKE A DATING AGENCY!"
Milton

"YOU KNOW WHAT PISSES ME OFF MOST ABOUT THIS PLACE? IT'S THE DAYS WHEN THERE AREN'T MANY CHICKS AROUND—ONLY "B" TEAM BROADS."

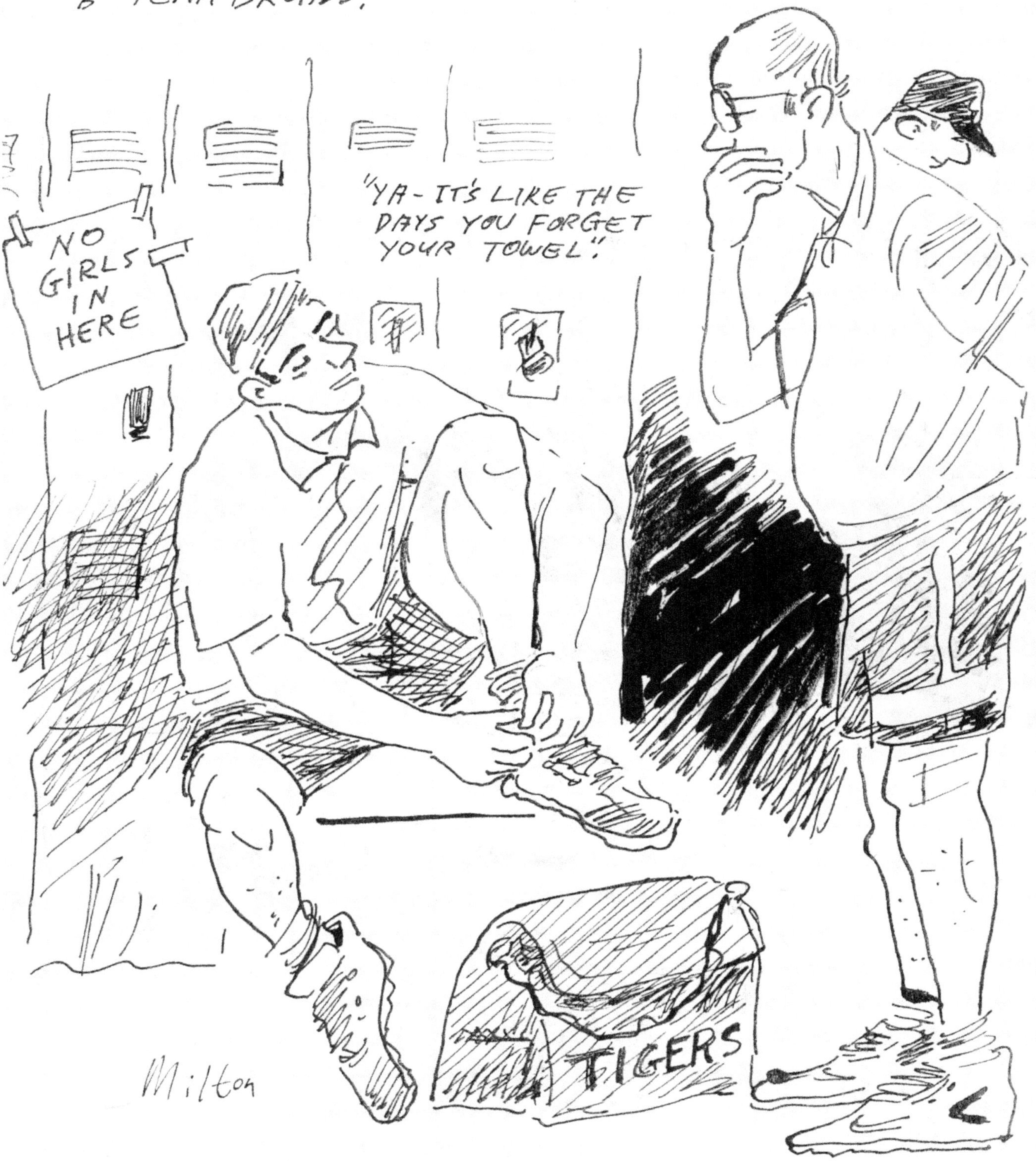
NO GIRLS IN HERE
"YA—IT'S LIKE THE DAYS YOU FORGET YOUR TOWEL."
TIGERS
Milton

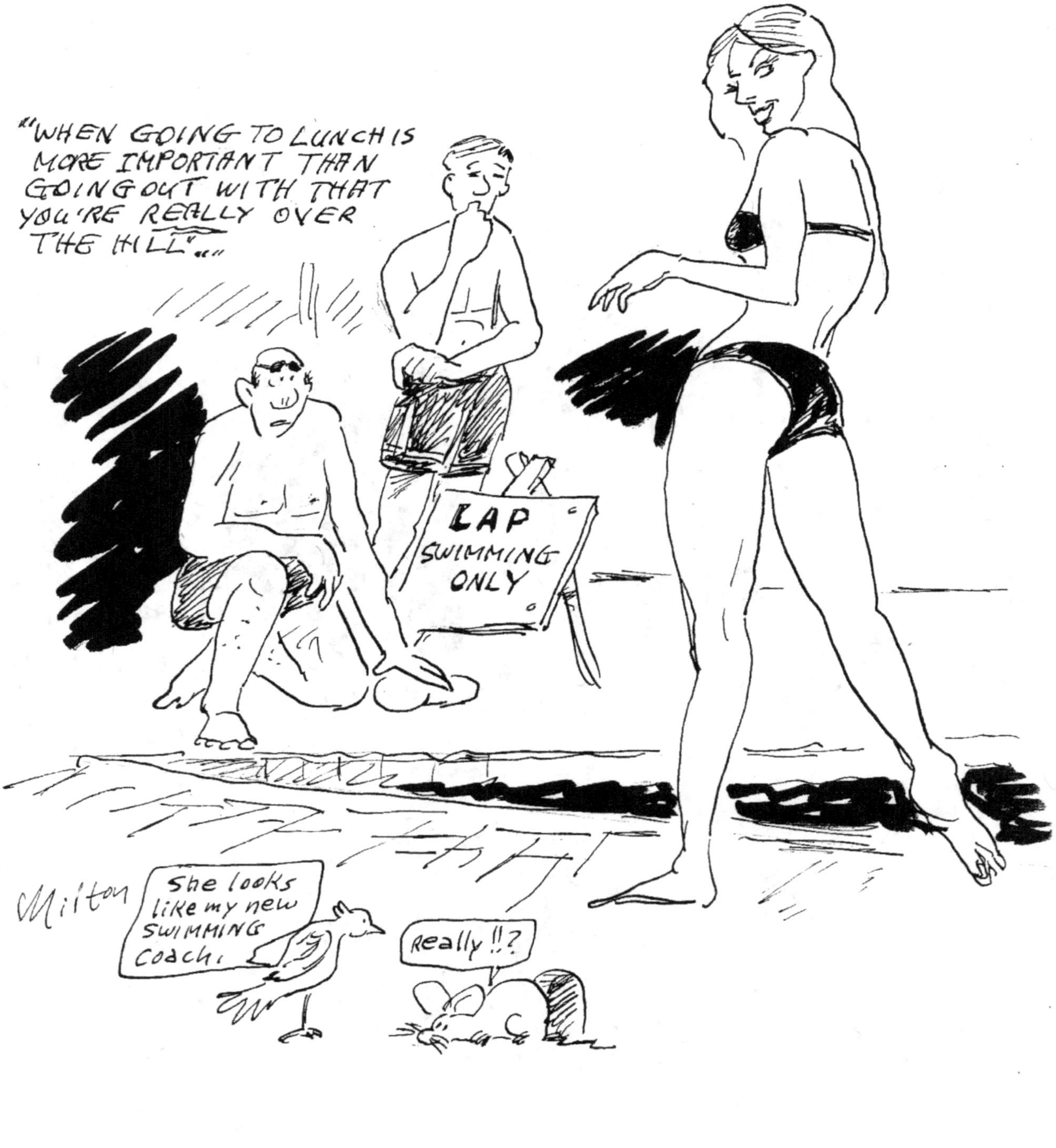
"WHEN GOING TO LUNCH IS MORE IMPORTANT THAN GOING OUT WITH THAT YOU'RE REALLY OVER THE HILL"..."
LAP SWIMMING ONLY
Milton
She looks like my new SWIMMING Coach.
Really !!?

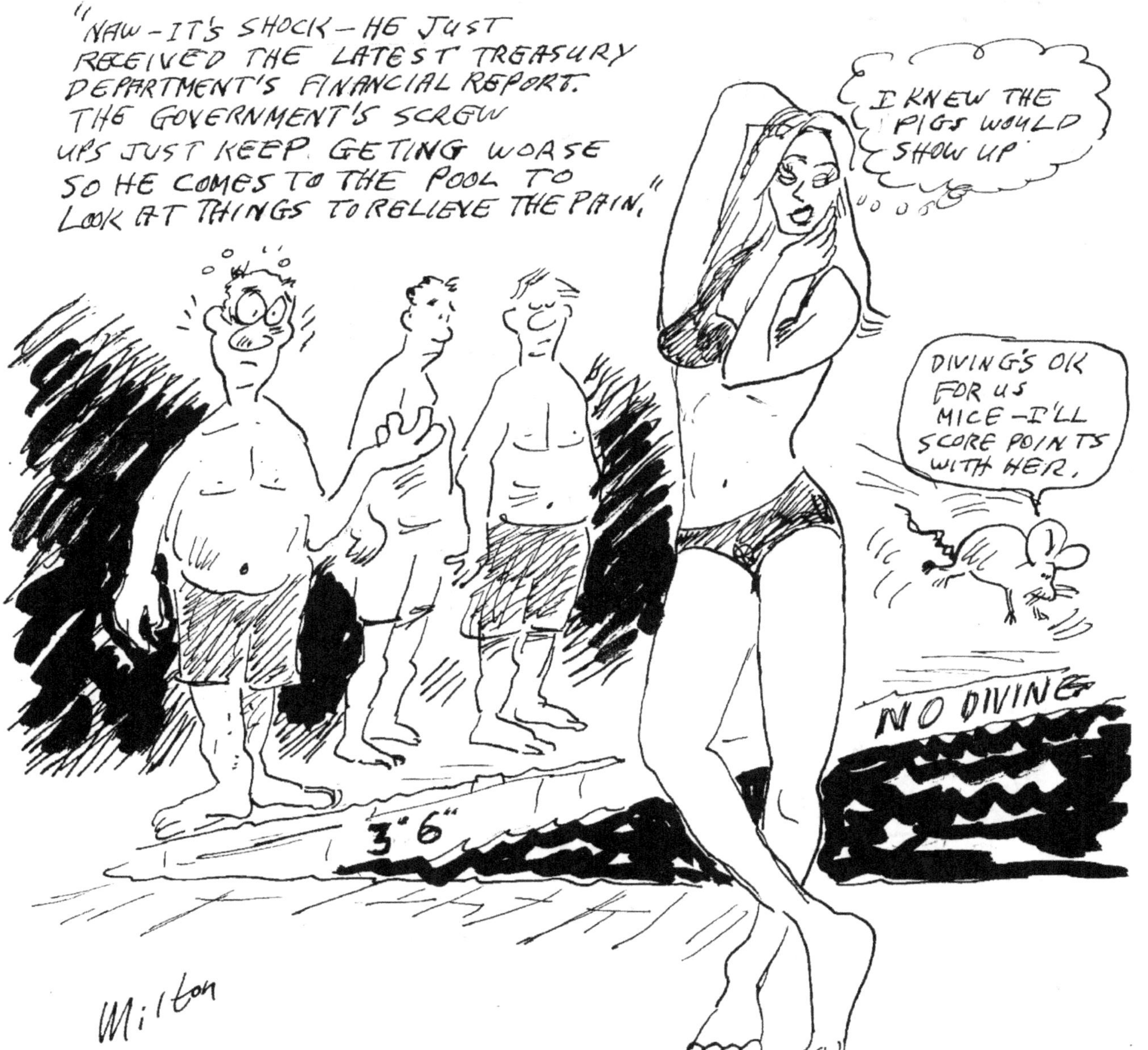
"NAW - IT'S SHOCK - HE JUST RECEIVED THE LATEST TREASURY DEPARTMENT'S FINANCIAL REPORT. THE GOVERNMENT'S SCREW UPS JUST KEEP GETING WORSE SO HE COMES TO THE POOL TO LOOK AT THINGS TO RELIEVE THE PAIN."
I KNEW THE PIGS WOULD SHOW UP
DIVING'S OK FOR US MICE - I'LL SCORE POINTS WITH HER.
NO DIVING
3'6"
Milton

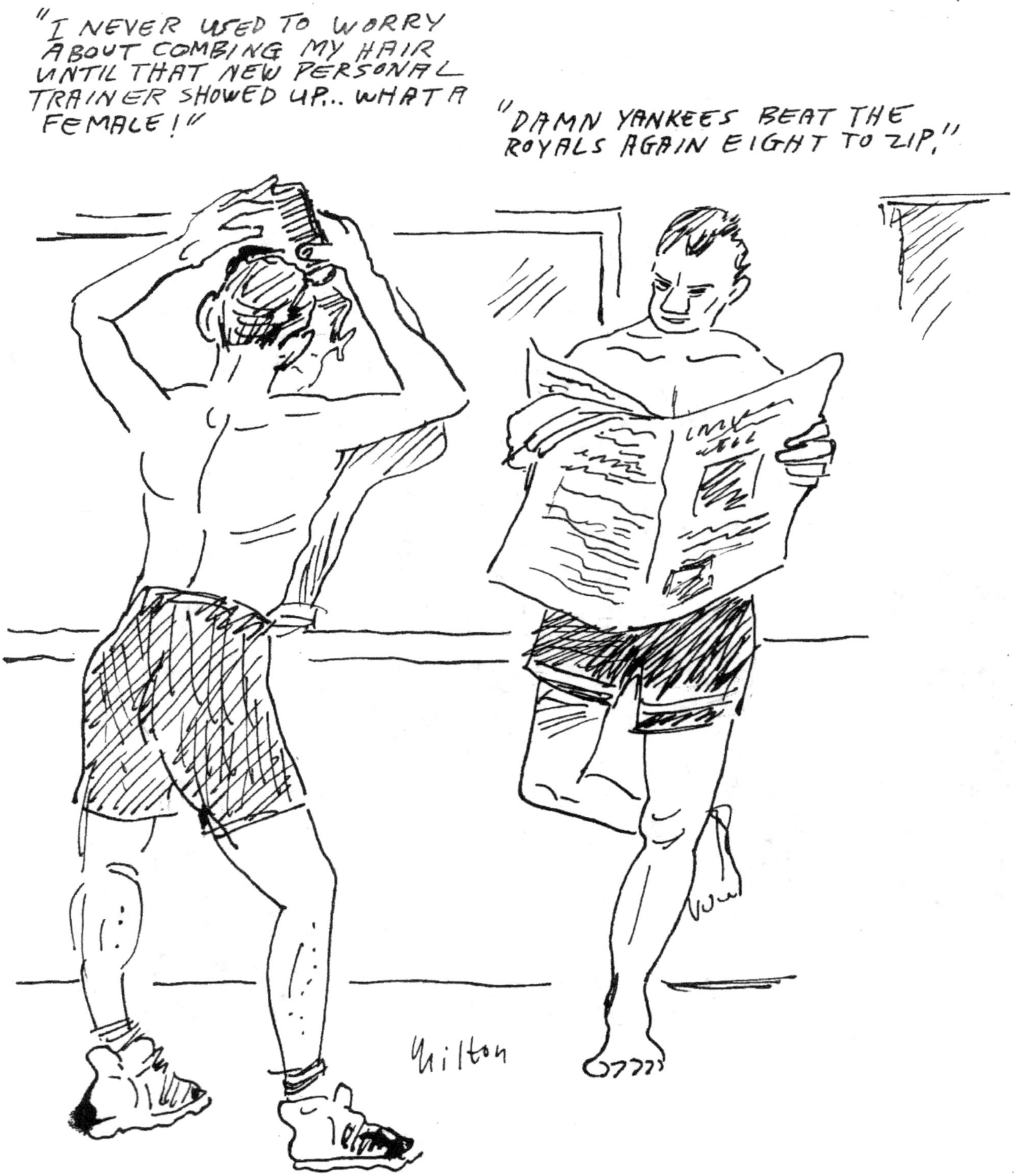
"I NEVER USED TO WORRY ABOUT COMBING MY HAIR UNTIL THAT NEW PERSONAL TRAINER SHOWED UP... WHAT A FEMALE!"
"DAMN YANKEES BEAT THE ROYALS AGAIN EIGHT TO ZIP."
Milton

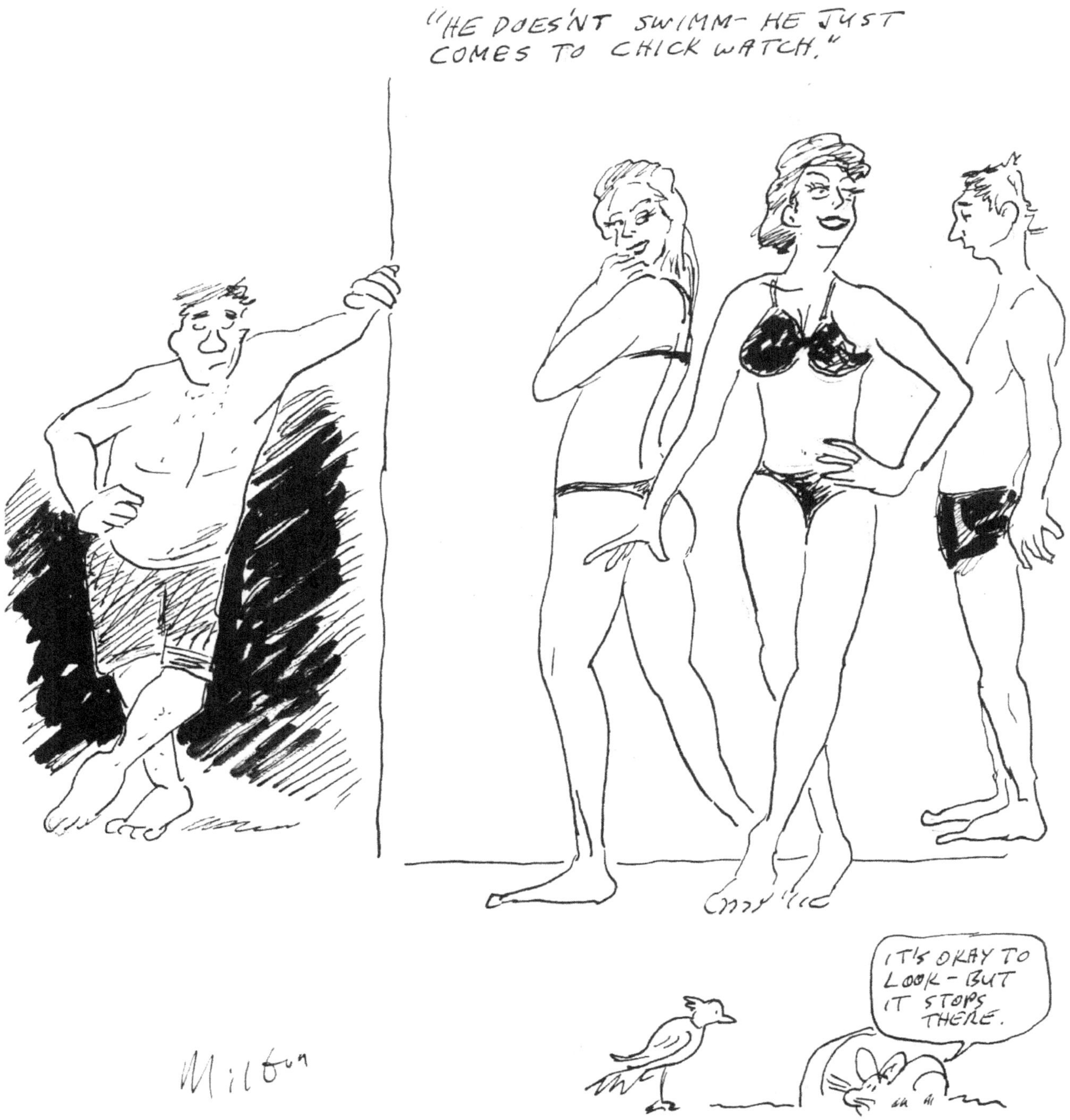
"HE DOES'NT SWIMM- HE JUST COMES TO CHICK WATCH."
IT'S OKAY TO LOOK - BUT IT STOPS THERE.
Milton

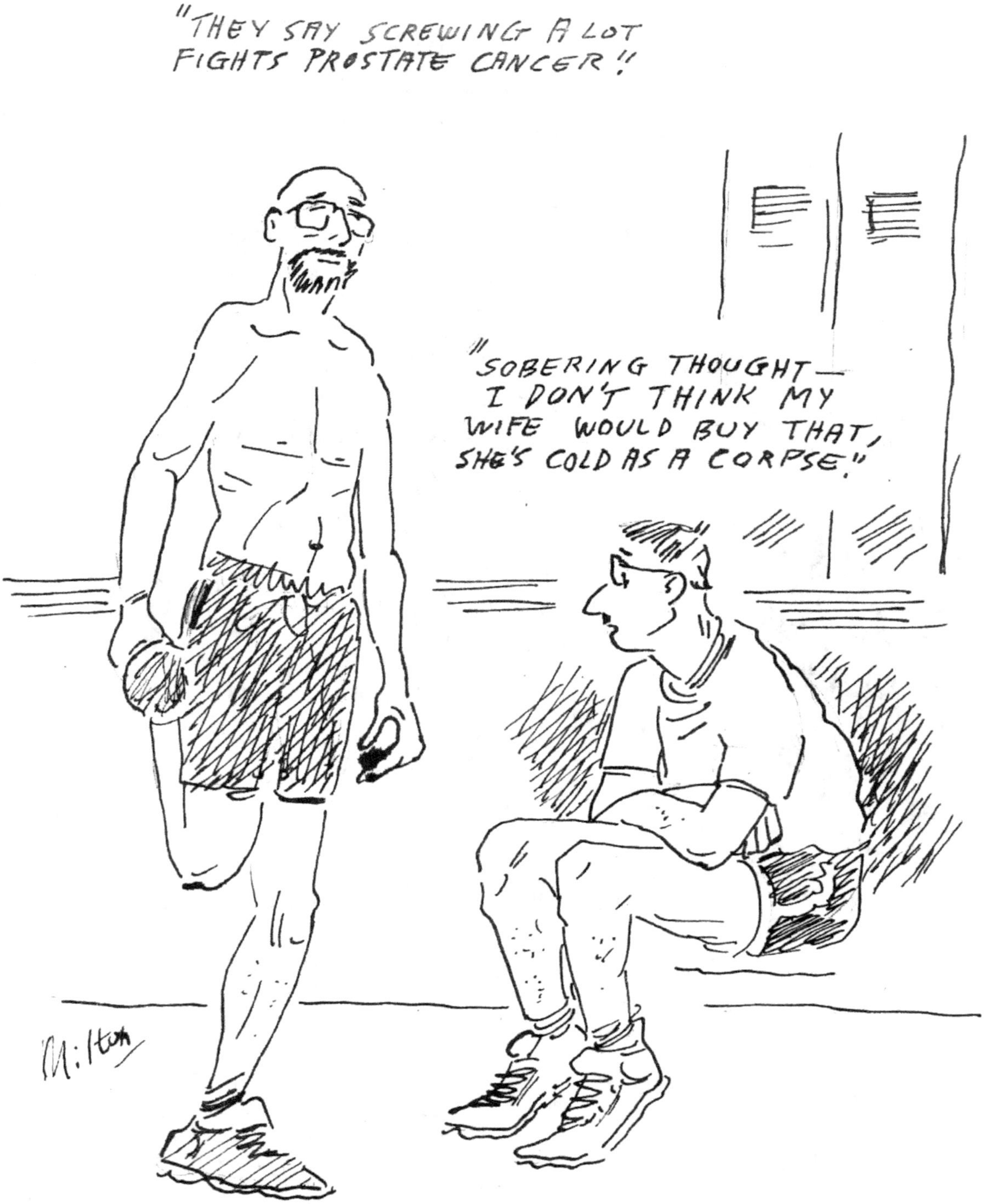
"THEY SAY SCREWING A LOT FIGHTS PROSTATE CANCER!"
"SOBERING THOUGHT— I DON'T THINK MY WIFE WOULD BUY THAT, SHE'S COLD AS A CORPSE."
Milton

www.ingramcontent.com/pod-product-compliance
Lightning Source LLC
Chambersburg PA
CBHW051420070526
44584CB00023B/3515